15-MINUTE
VEGETARIAN

15-MINUTE VEGETARIAN

200 QUICK, EASY, AND DELICIOUS RECIPES THE WHOLE FAMILY WILL LOVE

Susann Geiskopf-Hadler and Mindy Toomay

FAIR WINDS
PRESS
BEVERLY, MASSACHUSETTS

Text © 2005 by Susann Geiskopf-Hadler and Mindy Toomay

First published in the USA in 2006 by
Fair Winds Press, a member of
Quayside Publishing Group
100 Cummings Center
Suite 406-L
Beverly, MA 01915
www.fairwindspress.com

10 09 08   5 6 7 8

ISBN - 13: 978-1-59233-176-5
ISBN - 10: 1-59233-176-9

Library of Congress Cataloging-in-Publication Data
Geiskopf-Hadler, Susann, 1950-
  15-minute vegetarian recipes : 200 quick, easy, and delicious recipes the whole family will love /
Susann Geiskopf-Hadler with Mindy Toomay.
      p. cm.
  Summary: "Vegetarian recipes that can be made in fifteen minutes or less"--Provided by
publisher.
  Includes bibliographical references and index.
  ISBN 1-59233-176-9
 1. Vegetarian cookery. 2. Quick and easy cookery. I. Title: Fifteen-minute vegetarian recipes. II.
Toomay, Mindy, 1951- III. Title.
  TX837.G3793 2005
  641.5'636--dc22
                                                    2005023970

Cover design by Mary Ann Smith
Cover photograph by Allan Penn
Book design by Yee Design

Printed and bound in Canada

TABLE OF CONTENTS

INTRODUCTION

QUICK VEGETARIAN MEALS?

Is it possible to invent over 200 delicious, nutritious, and quick vegetarian dishes? After writing this book, we can answer that question with an unequivocal YES!

When we first embarked on the vegetarian path, it seemed we had a luxury of time. We set about inventing recipes based on whole, natural foods—grains and beans, fruits and vegetables, seeds and nuts, soy products, organic eggs and dairy products, and a world of seasonings—giving little consideration to how much time they would take to prepare. We were passionate cooks and enjoyed spending hours at a time in the kitchen.

But over the years, our lives became increasingly hectic. Along came careers, families, and a multitude of other commitments. Sound familiar? Busy as we were, however, we didn't want to give up the pleasures of preparing and sharing healthy home-cooked meals. That's why all of our previous collaborative cookbooks (and this is our eleventh!) have included "Almost Instant" recipes that require thirty minutes or less to prepare.

But could we make great dishes in half that time? Creating this cookbook challenged our quick-cooking skills, prompting us to explore the great selection of prepackaged ingredients now available in supermarkets. We found many that offer convenience without sacrificing good nutrition or flavor.

In these pages, we share our favorite discoveries with you, including plenty of tips that can save you time and trouble in the kitchen. Best of all, we provide a wide range of innovative recipes that achieve "from-scratch" results in a flash.

Now it's time to tie on an apron and enter the new age of quick vegetarian cooking.

CHAPTER ONE

READY, SET, COOK!

Even if you have only fifteen minutes to spend on meal preparation, you don't have to settle for a microwaved frozen dinner. With a little planning, some savvy shopping, and slight adjustments to your kitchen habits, you can turn out fresh and delicious breakfast, lunch, and dinner dishes—even luscious desserts—in mere minutes.

This chapter provides some tidbits of information that can help you become a happy and successful 15-minute cook.

Quick-Cooking Ground Rules

Fifteen minutes may not seem like a long time, but it's amazing what you can accomplish if you start with a well-stocked pantry and a great recipe. Here's what's included in our 15-minute preparation time:

- Dicing or mincing ingredients as called for in the recipe
- Measuring all ingredients
- Boiling water for cooking pasta or other purposes
- Preheating the broiler or gas grill
- Toasting nuts and seeds
- Garnishing and setting out finished dishes
- Cooking, from start to finish!

We took the liberty of excluding the following simple and basic tasks from the 15-minute time frame:

- Reading the recipe to fully grasp the cooking process before beginning

- Setting out all the ingredients called for in the recipe

- Setting out all necessary tools and equipment

- Chilling foods and beverages that are to be served cold

Our 15-minute time frame applies to people who are familiar with the most basic cooking tools and techniques. If you're just embarking on the cooking path, it may take you a few extra mintues to prepare our recipes.

That said, this is a great book for beginners, because it will introduce you to a wide variety of cooking styles and methods as you prepare very simple recipes. And don't forget: The more you practice, the faster you get!

Quick Cooking Tips and Techniques

You don't have to move at a frantic pace to prepare a 15-minute meal. An attitude of calm efficiency should be your modus operandi. Don't stress; enjoy the process. If you try the following tips, your cooking experience will feel almost effortless.

- Begin with a clean and uncluttered work surface and stove, which will help keep your mind clear and focused on each task.

- Before beginning to cook, read the recipe from start to finish, and visualize the cooking process as well as the finished dish.

- Set out all your ingredients and equipment before beginning to cook so you don't have to rummage in the spice cupboard or pantry at a crucial moment.

- If preparing more than one recipe for the same meal and they call for some of the same ingredients, stack functions by prepping all you need at the same time. For instance, if two recipes call for minced garlic, add up the number of cloves and mince them all at once.

- Place your garbage bin by the counter or place a large scrap bowl on the counter within arm's reach. This way, you won't waste time walking back and forth to the sink or trash bin to clear your work surface of vegetable parings and empty cans.

- Whenever you cook plain grains or beans, make extra and refrigerate or freeze the leftovers. (See Preparing Frequently Used Ingredients on page 234 for simple cooking instructions.)

- When prepping vegetables, chop more than you need for the recipe at hand and refrigerate the remainder in resealable plastic to use within a day or two.

- Organize your kitchen and pantry. Obviously, being able to immediately find what you're looking for is a great time-saver.

- Take the time on weekends to plan a few meals and do your shopping. This will save you enormous effort during the week, when you're likely to be on the run.

- When you use up the last bit of a particular staple, make a note of it so you'll remember to replenish your stock next time you go shopping.

- Stock your pantry with essential store-bought convenience foods that are great flavor enhancers, like salsa, pesto, marinara sauce, and roasted peppers. Better yet, use the simple recipes in Chapter 2, "Seasonings, Condiments, and Simple Sauces" (page 16), to make your own.

- Cook "hot." Don't be afraid of high temperatures. Just keep your eye on the pan so you can stir frequently and adjust the heat if it becomes necessary.

Slow-Cooked Flavor

When you're cooking in a 15-minute time frame, the following tricks used by professional cooks will maximize flavor with minimal effort.

- Keep whole spices on hand—such as nutmeg, cumin seeds, and peppercorns—and grind small amounts as needed.

- Toast spices, either whole or ground, in a dry pan for a few seconds to develop their flavors before adding them to the recipe.

- Dried herbs and spices contain volatile essential oils that deliver potent flavors, which diminish over time. Buy small quantities and replenish your supply frequently.

- Invest in superior oils and vinegars; they can elevate the flavor of a dish from ordinary to spectacular.

- Use fresh rather than prepackaged versions of certain essential flavor components. For instance, fresh-squeezed citrus juices and freshly minced garlic provide more satisfying flavor than their packaged counterparts.

Quick Cooking Tools and Equipment

As with every trade, the right tools can help you get the job of cooking done efficiently and with superior results. In developing recipes for this book, we used all the kitchen basics: a can opener, good knives and a steel for keeping them sharp, mixing bowls in various sizes, rubber and metal spatulas, sauté and sauce pans, a stockpot, wooden spoons, and various measuring spoons and cups. The following specialized tools also came into frequent service:

- Blender
- Cast-iron skillets in various sizes
- Citrus juicer, manual
- Citrus zester
- Coffee grinder
- Colanders and strainers in a variety of sizes

- Cutting boards in a variety of sizes
- Espresso machine
- Food processor
- Graters for specific purposes, such as cheese and ginger
- Grill, electric countertop model
- Grill, outdoor gas model
- Kitchen scale
- Mandoline or sharp box grater
- Melon baller
- Microplane zester and grater
- Microwave oven
- Mortar and pestle or spice grinder
- Salad spinner
- Steamer tray
- Toaster oven
- Tongs
- Vegetable peeler
- Whisk
- Wok

Classic Cast-Iron

Newly manufactured cast-iron pans are available at kitchen stores, but you can also find them at flea markets, thrift stores, or garage sales. Since cast-iron is practically indestructible, these vintage pans are as good as new, and may already be perfectly "seasoned" by the previous owner. If they're rusty, scrub well and proceed with seasoning as for a new cast-iron pan, which creates a stick-free surface. Simply rub the pan well with vegetable oil, leaving no residual oil in the pan. Heat over medium heat on your stovetop or in your oven for several minutes, then allow to cool. Repeat this procedure two or three more times and you can begin cooking with your seasoned cast-iron pan. Wash cast-iron pans briefly with soapy water and dry immediately so no rust forms. Don't scrub at the pan with steel wool or another abrasive material—you don't want to remove that "seasoning" layer.

When you've finished cooking the meal, you'll want to use attractive serving pieces: bowls and platters, dessert dishes, beverage glasses, and dinnerware.

Put some creativity into setting the mood with a pretty table, and you and your family and friends will enjoy the food even more. Place mats, cloth napkins and napkin rings, your favorite flatware, candles in interesting holders, vases full of fresh flowers—these take only a few moments to set out but greatly enhance everyone's dining experience.

Time for a toast: To good health and long life!

CHAPTER TWO

SEASONINGS, CONDIMENTS, AND SIMPLE SAUCES

This chapter presents flavorful and easy-to-prepare salad dressings, salsas, sauces, and condiments. Many of them are called for as ingredients in other recipes throughout this book.

You can purchase ready-made versions of some of the basics, such as basil pesto or tofu mayonnaise, but you will enjoy better taste and consume fewer chemical additives if you whip them up at home.

They also can be easier on your food budget. Homemade salad dressings, for instance, are more economical than their store-bought counterparts and can spark up sandwiches and steamed vegetables as well as mixed greens.

Prepare these recipes over the weekend, when you're likely to have more leisure time for cooking. Use immediately or store leftovers in tightly closed containers in the refrigerator.

If you haven't tapped the creative potential of simple homemade sauces, make up a batch of Basil Pesto (page 23), Tomato Marinara Sauce (page 25), or Miso Tahini Sauce (page 23), which all have countless uses. They're great tossed with pasta, grains, and raw or cooked vegetables, for instance.

Make the recipes in this chapter your quick-cooking allies. You will use and enjoy them often!

USE THESE TIPS TO GET FABULOUS, FULL-BODIED FLAVOR
FROM YOUR SALAD DRESSINGS, SAUCES, AND SPICES.

A great vinaigrette depends on good
olive oil; buy the best quality you can
afford. It will repay you with excellent
flavor and health benefits.

Vinaigrettes may be whisked up in a bowl, as
described in our recipes, or the ingredients
can be combined in a jar with a tight lid and
shaken vigorously until emulsified.

Vinaigrettes and some sauces tend
to solidify when chilled. Return to room
temperature and shake or whisk to
recombine the ingredients before using.

Plan on 1 to 2 tablespoons of
salad dressing or sauce per person,
depending on personal taste.

Herb and spice blends should be stored
in tightly capped jars in a cool, dark cupboard. The volatile oils in these flavor
enhancers quickly oxidize when exposed
to light, heat, or air.

 VEGAN

Red Wine Vinaigrette

This is a classic vinaigrette. You can make a
hundred variations on it by using different
vinegars or adding fresh herbs or other
savory ingredients, such as capers or
Parmesan cheese.

Ingredients
1 teaspoon dried basil
1/2 teaspoon dried oregano
2 tablespoons (28 ml) red wine vinegar
1/2 cup (120 ml) extra-virgin olive oil
1/2 teaspoon granulated sugar
1/2 teaspoon granulated garlic
1/2 teaspoon Dijon mustard
1/8 teaspoon salt
Several grinds black pepper

Combine the basil and oregano in the palm
of one hand and lightly crush the dried
herbs with your fingers. Place them in a
bowl and add the red wine vinegar, olive oil,
sugar, garlic, mustard, salt, and pepper.
Whisk until emulsified, about 1 minute.

Yield: 3/4 cup (175 ml)
PER TABLESPOON: 82 calories; 9 g fat; trace protein;
.5 g carbohydrate; trace dietary fiber; 0 mg cholesterol.

VEGAN

Meyer Lemon Vinaigrette

This light dressing is tasty on fresh salad greens or steamed vegetables. If you're not using the Meyer lemon variety, you may need to add a bit more sugar.

Ingredients

1 teaspoon oregano
$^3/_4$ cup (175 ml) extra-virgin olive oil
$^1/_4$ cup (60 ml) freshly squeezed lemon juice
1 teaspoon crushed garlic
$^1/_2$ teaspoon granulated sugar
Pinch salt
Several grinds black pepper

Place the oregano in the palm of one hand and lightly crush it with your fingers. Place it in a bowl and add the olive oil, lemon juice, garlic, sugar, salt, and pepper. Whisk until emulsified, about 1 minute.

Yield: 1 cup (235 ml)
PER TABLESPOON: 92 calories; 10 g fat; trace protein; 1 g carbohydrate; trace dietary fiber; 0 mg cholesterol.

Umami Power

Utilize the power of umami, which is now widely accepted as a fifth basic taste—meaning our taste buds can recognize it as a distinct flavor, just as they recognize sweet, salty, sour, and bitter. Good examples of deeply savory umami foods are dried mushrooms, aged blue cheese, and soy sauce. Using them in a dish creates a rich, satisfying flavor.

Raspberry Vinaigrette

This vinaigrette is especially good with mixed greens and goat cheese.

Ingredients

$^1/_2$ cup (120 ml) raspberry vinegar
$^1/_4$ cup (60 ml) extra-virgin olive oil
$^1/_4$ cup (60 g) mayonnaise
2 tablespoons (40 g) honey
Several grinds black pepper

Place vinegar, olive oil, mayonnaise, honey, and pepper in a bowl and whisk until emulsified, about 1 minute.

Yield: 1 cup (235 ml)
PER TABLESPOON: 64 calories; 6 g fat; trace protein; 3 g carbohydrate; trace dietary fiber; 1 mg cholesterol.

Tomato Balsamic Vinaigrette

This vinaigrette will liven up any leafy salad or a pasta and veggie melange. Because it's based on tomatoes, the oil content is lower than usual, making it a good reduced-fat choice.

Ingredients

$1/2$ cup (120 g) canned diced tomatoes, undrained
$1/4$ cup (60 ml) extra-virgin olive oil
$1/4$ cup (60 ml) balsamic vinegar
1 teaspoon crushed garlic
$1/2$ teaspoon salt
Several grinds black pepper

Combine all ingredients in a blender and puree until emulsified.

Yield: $3/4$ cup (175 ml)
PER TABLESPOON: 43 calories; 5 g fat; trace protein; 1 g carbohydrate; trace dietary fiber; 0 mg cholesterol.

Blue Cheese Dressing

This smooth, reduced-fat version of the universal favorite is tangy and cheesy, with just the right garlic note. Try it as a sandwich spread as well as a salad dressing. If the refrigerated dressing becomes too thick to pour, thin it out with a drizzle of water as needed.

Ingredients

4 ounces (115 g) blue cheese, crumbled
$2/3$ cup (160 g) plain nonfat yogurt
2 tablespoons (30 g) mayonnaise
1 tablespoon (15 ml) cider vinegar
2 teaspoons crushed garlic
Several grinds black pepper
$1/8$ teaspoon salt

Combine the blue cheese, yogurt, mayonnaise, vinegar, garlic, black pepper, and salt in a blender and process until smooth.

Yield: $1^1/2$ cups (370 g)
PER TABLESPOON: 29 calories; 2 g fat; 1 g protein; 1 g carbohydrate; trace dietary fiber; 4 mg cholesterol.

Light Crème Fraîche

This slightly thinned sour cream topping mimics the taste and texture of traditional cultured crème fraîche. It is very simple to make and can be used as a condiment on tortilla dishes, cooked vegetables, even desserts. It will stay fresh in the refrigerator for a few days.

Ingredients

1 cup (230 g) lowfat sour cream

$^1/_4$ cup (60 ml) half-and-half

Whisk the sour cream and half-and-half together in a bowl. Transfer to a jar and refrigerate.

Yield: 1$^1/_4$ cups (295 g)

PER TABLESPOON: 8 calories; 1 g fat; trace protein; 1 g carbohydrate; 0 g dietary fiber; 2 mg cholesterol.

Mayonnaise

Easy to make, this mayonnaise is delicious, and cholesterol-free. You can add fresh herbs such as cilantro, basil, or oregano to make a flavored mayonnaise. The consistency is stiffer than traditional mayo, but it can be used for all the same purposes.

Ingredients

2 large egg whites

1 teaspoon crushed garlic

$^1/_4$ teaspoon salt

$^1/_2$ cup (120 ml) extra-virgin olive oil

Place the egg whites, garlic, and salt in a blender. With the blender on, add the olive oil in a slow, steady stream and process until emulsified, about 1 minute.

Yield: $^2/_3$ cup (150 g)

PER TABLESPOON: 90 calories; 10 g fat; 1 g protein; trace carbohydrate; trace dietary fiber; 0 mg cholesterol.

Tofu Mayonnaise

This soy-based condiment delivers a dose of healthy monounsaturated fats instead of the saturated kind found in regular mayo. Use it in sandwiches, on steamed vegetables, or in salad dressings. If the mayonnaise separates while stored in the refrigerator, simply whisk to recombine.

Ingredients

12 ounces (340 g) firm silken tofu
3 tablespoons (45 ml) freshly squeezed
   lemon juice
2 tablespoons (28 ml) extra-virgin olive oil
1 teaspoon dry mustard
$1/2$ teaspoon salt

Combine the tofu, lemon juice, olive oil, mustard, and salt in a blender and puree until emulsified, about 1 minute.

Yield: 1$1/2$ cups (340 g)
PER TABLESPOON: 22 calories; 2 g fat; 1 g protein; 1 g carbohydrate; trace dietary fiber; 0 mg cholesterol.

Cilantro Aioli

This makes a fantastic dipping sauce for artichokes or raw veggie sticks and is also a great sandwich spread (see Southwest Tofu Club Sandwich on page 106). Tofu mayo, sometimes called by a special brand name, is available at natural food stores and some supermarkets, or use our homemade version, see left.

Ingredients

1 cup tofu mayonnaise
2 cups (120 g) lightly packed coarsely
   chopped fresh cilantro
1 tablespoon (15 ml) freshly squeezed
   lime juice
3 cloves garlic, coarsely chopped
$1/4$ teaspoon salt
Several grinds black pepper

Place the mayonnaise in the blender, then add the cilantro, lime juice, garlic, salt, and pepper. Puree. Store in a tightly closed container in the refrigerator and use within about 2 weeks.

Yield: 2 cups
PER TABLESPOON: 22 calories; 1 g fat; 1 g protein; 2 g carbohydrate; trace dietary fiber; 0 mg cholesterol.

VEGAN

Basil Pesto

Plant some basil in your garden or even in pots in the spring to reap a harvest starting in the late summer. You may use this pesto immediately, or make up a big batch and freeze it for a taste of summer during the winter. Place a slice of lemon over the top of the pesto before securing the lid. Be sure to leave at least a quarter inch of headspace at the top of the jar, as the pesto will expand as it freezes.

Ingredients

2 cups (90 g) fresh basil leaves, loosely
    packed
$1/3$ cup (80 ml) extra-virgin olive oil,
    divided
$1/4$ cup (35 g) pine nuts
6 cloves garlic, minced
$3/4$ cup (75 g) grated Parmesan cheese

Before measuring, wash the basil, discarding any thick stems, and dry thoroughly. In a food processor or blender, puree the basil with $1/4$ cup (60 ml) of the olive oil, the pine nuts, garlic, and Parmesan cheese until thick and homogeneous. With the machine running, add the remaining olive oil in a thin, steady stream to form a smooth paste.

Yield: 1 cup (260 g)
PER TABLESPOON: 72 calories; 7 g fat; 2 g protein; 1 g carbohydrate; trace dietary fiber; 3 mg cholesterol.

 VEGAN

Miso Tahini Sauce

This sauce is wonderful on baked potatoes or any cooked grain or vegetable. We especially recommend it on beets. Use immediately, or store in a tightly closed container in the refrigerator for up to 2 weeks and reheat before using.

Ingredients

$1/3$ cup (90 g) light-colored miso
$1/4$ cup (60 g) sesame tahini
$1/4$ cup (60 ml) freshly squeezed
    lemon juice
1 teaspoon crushed garlic
$1/8$ teaspoon cayenne pepper

Put $3/4$ cup (175 ml) water on to boil over high heat. Place the miso and tahini in a medium bowl and mash together with a fork. Add the lemon juice and mash until it is well combined. Now add the boiling water a little at a time, whisking to incorporate. When all the water has been added, whisk in the garlic and cayenne until smooth.

Yield: 1½ cups (355 ml)
PER TABLESPOON: 24 calories; 2 g fat; 1 g protein; 2 g carbohydrate; trace dietary fiber; 0 mg cholesterol.

Asian Peanut Sauce

Here is a deliciously exotic sauce for steamed veggies, tofu or tempeh, whole grains, or noodles—or any combination of the above! Use immediately, or store it in a tightly closed container in the refrigerator for up to 2 weeks. The chili sauce called for in the recipe is sold in squeeze bottles in the ethnic foods section of many large supermarkets and in Asian specialty stores. Increase the amount for a spicier version.

Ingredients

$^1/_4$ cup (65 g) creamy peanut butter

2 tablespoons (28 ml) freshly squeezed lime juice

$1^1/_2$ tablespoons (25 ml) soy sauce

1 tablespoon (15 g) granulated sugar

2 teaspoons hot Asian chili sauce

1 teaspoon crushed garlic

$^1/_8$ teaspoon salt

Whisk together the peanut butter, lime juice, soy sauce, sugar, chili sauce, garlic, and salt, along with 2 tablespoons (28 ml) water, until smooth.

Yield: About $^2/_3$ cup (160 ml)

PER TABLESPOON: 42 calories; 3 g fat; 2 g protein; 3 g carbohydrate; trace dietary fiber; 0 mg cholesterol.

Tomato Marinara Sauce

Over the years, you will come up with many tasty variations on this basic sauce. A tablespoon or two of chopped capers or olives, for instance, adds a distinctive flavor. Use this sauce as a topping for pasta, grains, eggs, or veggies. Plan on about 1/4 cup (65 g) per serving.

Leftovers can be stored in the refrigerator in a tightly closed container to be enjoyed over the course of a week or so. If you don't have any red wine open, substitute white wine, sherry, or even port.

Ingredients

2 tablespoons (28 ml) extra-virgin olive oil

2 cloves garlic, minced

1 can (28 ounces, or 785 g) crushed tomatoes, undrained

2 tablespoons (60 ml) red wine

1 tablespoon Italian herb seasoning (see page 28)

1/2 teaspoon salt

1/4 teaspoon coarsely ground black pepper

Heat the oil in a skillet over medium-high heat and stir and sauté the garlic in the hot oil until it is light tan, about 30 seconds. Add the tomatoes, red wine, Italian seasoning, salt, and pepper, and bring to a simmer. Reduce the heat to medium and simmer, stirring frequently, until reduced to a medium sauce consistency, about 5 minutes.

Yield: 2¹/₂ cups (750 g)

PER 1/4 CUP (65 G): 38 calories; 2 g fat; 1 g protein; 3 g carbohydrate; 1 g dietary fiber; 0 mg cholesterol.

Salsa Fresca

The ingredients for this salsa are at their peak during the summer months but are also available year-round in most areas. This salsa is great with corn chips. If your skin is really sensitive, wear surgical gloves for handling the jalapeño. If you do get jalapeño juice on your fingers, be sure not to rub your eyes or touch other sensitive areas. Leftovers keep well. Store them in a tightly closed container in the refrigerator for up to a week or so.

Ingredients

3 large plum tomatoes

1 medium jalapeño pepper

1 tablespoon (15 ml) olive oil

$^1/_4$ cup (60 ml) freshly squeezed lemon juice

2 tablespoons minced fresh cilantro

$^1/_2$ teaspoon crushed garlic

Pinch salt

Cut the plum tomatoes in half crosswise and squeeze them gently over the sink to remove the juicy seed pockets. Dice the tomatoes and place in a medium bowl. Remove the stem of the jalapeño pepper and cut it in half lengthwise. Use a teaspoon to scrape out and discard the seeds. Finely mince the jalapeño and add it to the tomatoes. Add the olive oil, lemon juice, cilantro, garlic, and salt. Stir until well combined.

Yield: 1$^1/_2$ cups (340 g)

PER $^1/_4$ CUP (65 G): 32 calories; 2 g fat; trace protein; 3 g carbohydrate; 1 g dietary fiber; 0 mg cholesterol.

Smooth Chipotle Chile Salsa

Medium-hot on the spicy scale, this simple salsa is made with chipotle chiles canned in *adobo* sauce, which are available in most supermarkets and any Mexican specialty market.

Ingredients

1 cup (240 g) canned diced tomatoes, drained

2/3 cup (110 g) diced white onion

2 tablespoons (32 g) tomato paste

1 tablespoon (15 ml) freshly squeezed lime juice

2 medium *chipotle chiles en adobo*, diced

2 teaspoons adobo sauce (from canned chipotle chiles)

2 teaspoons ground cumin

2 teaspoons crushed garlic

Place the tomatoes, onion, tomato paste, lime juice, chiles en adobo, adobo sauce, cumin, and garlic in a blender or food processor and pulse until smooth.

Yield: 1 3/4 cups (395 g)

PER TABLESPOON (65 G): 31 calories; 1 g fat; 1 g protein; 5 g carbohydrate; 1 g dietary fiber; trace cholesterol.

Smooth Cilantro Salsa

This thin puree can spark up any number of dishes, and a little bit goes a long way. It is particularly good with potatoes, beans, or eggs.

Ingredients

1 cup (60 g) chopped fresh cilantro
2 tablespoons (28 ml) extra-virgin olive oil
2 teaspoons freshly squeezed lemon juice
$1/4$ teaspoon ground coriander
$1/8$ teaspoon pure chili powder
Pinch salt

Place the cilantro in a food processor and pulse to chop. In a small bowl, whisk together the olive oil, lemon juice, coriander, chili powder, and salt. Add to the cilantro and puree.

Yield: $1/4$ cup (60 ml)
PER TABLESPOON: 62 calories; 7 g fat; trace protein; trace carbohydrate; trace dietary fiber; 0 mg cholesterol.

Italian Herb Seasoning

This blend is perfect for soups, tomato sauces, salad dressing, and marinades. Store it in a tightly covered jar in a dark cupboard. It will stay fresh and flavorful for about 6 months.

Ingredients

3 tablespoons dried basil
2 tablespoons dried oregano
2 tablespoons dried parsley
1 tablespoon dried rosemary

Combine the herbs and lightly crush them, using a spice grinder or a mortar and pestle. (Do this in two or more batches, if necessary, so your ingredients don't overflow.)

Yield: About $1/2$ cup (16 g)
PER TABLESPOON: 0 calories; trace fat; trace protein; 2 g carbohydrate; 1 g dietary fiber; 0 mg cholesterol.

Herbes de Provence

This classic French seasoning can be used in soups, vegetable sautés, marinades, or anywhere you want a mild and aromatic herb flavor. Store it in a tightly covered jar in a dark cupboard. It will stay fresh and flavorful for about 6 months.

Ingredients

1 tablespoon fennel seeds

2 tablespoons dried oregano

2 tablespoons dried thyme

1 tablespoon dried lavender flowers

1 tablespoon dried rosemary

1 tablespoon dried tarragon

Lightly crush the fennel seeds, using a spice grinder or mortar and pestle. Transfer them to a bowl, add all the herbs, and stir until well combined.

Yield: About ½ cup (16 g)

PER TABLESPOON: 13 calories; trace fat; 1 g protein; 3 g carbohydrate; 2 g dietary fiber; 0 mg cholesterol.

Curry Powder

Curry powder has so many uses, and making your own allows you to control the heat. This recipe makes a rather mild blend. Like it extra spicy? Add more cayenne pepper. Store it in a tightly covered jar in a dark cupboard. It will stay fresh and flavorful for about 6 months.

Ingredients

2½ tablespoons ground ginger

2½ tablespoons ground coriander

1½ tablespoons ground turmeric

1½ tablespoons ground cumin

2 teaspoons ground cinnamon

2 teaspoons ground cloves

2 teaspoons cayenne pepper

Place all the spices in a bowl and stir until well combined.

Yield: About ½ cup (55 g)

PER TEASPOON: 8 calories; trace fat; trace protein; 1 g carbohydrate; trace dietary fiber; 0 mg cholesterol.

CHAPTER THREE

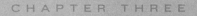

15-MINUTE
BREAKFAST
DISHES

Some people wake up ravenous, while for some it may take an hour or so to really get in the mood for food. Still others could easily skip the morning meal altogether, but that's a mistake. Most health experts call breakfast the most important meal of the day because it establishes steady energy production and prevents overeating later on. Paradoxically, skipping breakfast is more likely to contribute to weight gain than to weight loss.

The morning meals in this chapter were created to satisfy a variety of appetites. From smoothies to porridge to high-protein egg and tofu preparations, these dishes cover all the bases. And they're ready to eat in just fifteen minutes, so even the most harried among us have time for a satisfying breakfast before rushing off to work.

Some are special enough to showcase at a weekend brunch, such as Poached Eggs on a Bed of Sautéed Spinach (page 45), Cottage Cheese Pancakes (page 38), and Curried Tofu Scramble with Roasted Peppers and Peas (page 41). Add juice, tea, or coffee; a platter of sliced fruit; and a basketful of store-bought scones or muffins. Your guests will be delighted to loll away part of the day at your table.

THESE TIPS WILL HELP YOU ENJOY
BREAKFAST EVEN MORE.

We always buy organic free-range
eggs, which provide superior flavor
and nutrition.

You may want to add special health
boosters to your smoothies, such as
ground flaxseed, spirulina powder, or
ascorbic acid (vitamin C) powder.
Health food stores carry special nutrient
mixes and protein powders for just
this purpose. If you use them, read the
labels and be careful to avoid any
strange-sounding additives.

Immediately after serving up a batch of
porridge, soak its cooking pot in water.
Otherwise, the starchy bits of porridge
that remain in the pot will stick like glue
as they dry.

Breakfast is a great time to load up
on fiber. Whole grain cereals, fresh and
dried fruit, and nuts and seeds are
high-fiber foods that can help you
meet your daily requirement.

Blueberry Flax Smoothie

Flaxseed, available in natural food stores
and many major supermarkets, is a great
source of the important omega-3 fatty
acids and beneficial dietary fiber. Here is a
delicious way to enjoy your daily dose.

Ingredients

$1^1/_4$ cups (305 g) plain nonfat yogurt

1 cup (155 g) frozen blueberries

1 banana, peeled and cut into chunks

2 tablespoons (15 g) whole or freshly
    ground flaxseed

Combine the yogurt, blueberries, banana,
and flaxseed in a blender and process until
smooth.

Yield: 2 servings

Each will have: 227 calories; 4 g fat; 12 g protein; 38 g
carbohydrate; 6 g dietary fiber; 3 mg cholesterol.

Aloha Smoothie

This rich smoothie delivers a lot of health promoting enzymes in addition to great taste. It is delicious at room temperature, but feel free to chill the ingredients ahead of time if you want a cold beverage.

Ingredients

1 1/2 cups (210 g) chopped fresh or canned papaya (packed in juice)

1 small banana, sliced

1/2 cup (120 ml) light coconut milk

1/2 cup (120 ml) plain rice milk

1 tablespoon (15 ml) freshly squeezed lime juice

Put the papaya in the blender with the banana, coconut milk, rice milk, and lime juice. Process until smooth.

Yield: 4 servings

Each will have: 133 calories; 8 g fat; 1 g protein; 17 g carbohydrate; 2 g dietary fiber; 0 mg cholesterol.

No Time for Breakfast?

Being rushed in the morning is no excuse to skip breakfast. If you keep a few healthy staples on hand, you can grab a quick bite as you dash for the door. Here are some super-simple suggestions:

- Sprouted-grain English muffin with nut butter and sliced bananas

- Leftover brown rice with a splash of low-fat milk and a handful of berries

- Plain lowfat yogurt with all-fruit preserves and a sprinkling of granola

- Rye crackers spread with goat cheese and a dab of orange marmalade

- Soy milk in the blender with frozen fruit, flaxseed, and a drizzle of honey

Strawberry Soy Smoothie with Mint

There's no tastier—or simpler—way to enjoy the health benefits of strawberries and soy than this refreshing smoothie. If you can find fresh, in-season berries at your local market, by all means use them, cutting out their stem ends with a sharp paring knife before placing them in the blender. If strawberries aren't in season, however, frozen berries may be more flavorful than fresh. Both work well in this recipe.

Ingredients

2 cups (300 g) fresh or frozen whole
    strawberries
1¹/₄ cups (295 ml) vanilla soy milk
6 large fresh mint leaves, or more, to taste
1 teaspoon maple syrup, if desired

Combine the strawberries, soy milk, and mint in a blender and process until smooth and frothy. Taste, and add maple syrup if you want a sweeter smoothie.

Yield: 2 servings

Each will have: 259 calories; 3 g fat; 6 g protein; 59 g carbohydrate; 7 g dietary fiber; 0 mg cholesterol.

Oat and Apple Porridge with Raisins

Nothing could be more satisfying than a bowl of hot oatmeal on a chilly morning. This one increases the good-health quotient with apple and raisins. You may garnish the finished porridge with the milk of your choice, more maple syrup, and chopped nuts, if you wish.

Ingredients

1 cup (80 g) quick-cooking rolled oats
Pinch of salt
1 medium apple
2 tablespoons (20 g) raisins
1 tablespoon (15 ml) maple syrup

Combine the oats with the salt and 1 cup (235 ml) water in a saucepan over medium-high heat. Dice the apple, discarding the core, and add it to the oats, along with the raisins. Cover, reduce the heat to low, and cook 5 minutes. Stir in the maple syrup and serve.

Yield: 2 servings

Each will have: 236 calories; 3 g fat; 5 g protein; 47 g carbohydrate; 5 g dietary fiber; 0 mg cholesterol.

Oat and Pear Porridge
with Ginger and Raisins

This great combination of flavors is a nice change from ordinary oatmeal.

Ingredients

1 cup (80 g) rolled oats

Pinch of salt

1 medium pear, unpeeled, any variety

2 tablespoons (20 g) raisins

$^1/_2$ teaspoon ground ginger

1 cup (235 ml) lowfat milk

1 tablespoon (15 ml) maple syrup

Combine the oats with the salt and 2 cups (475 ml) water in a saucepan over medium-high heat. Dice the pear, discarding the core, and add it to the oats, along with the raisins and ginger. Cover, reduce the heat to low, and cook 5 minutes. Turn off the heat and allow to stand without disturbing the lid for 2 minutes.

Transfer equal portions of the porridge to individual serving bowls. Pour $^1/_2$ cup (120 ml) milk over each serving and drizzle with $^1/_2$ tablespoon of maple syrup.

Yield: 2 servings

Each will have: 310 calories; 4 g fat; 11 g protein; 60 g carbohydrate; 7 g dietary fiber; 5 mg cholesterol.

VEGAN

Brown Rice and Pear Porridge

Brown rice makes a delicious porridge, but you could substitute cooked bulgur wheat, barley, or kasha if you happen to have some on hand. You will leave the breakfast table feeling energized for a productive morning. Feel free to substitute dairy or soy milk for the rice milk.

Ingredients

1 large pear

$1^1/_2$ cups (290 g) cooked brown rice

$1^1/_2$ cups (355 ml) rice milk

3 tablespoons (30 g) raisins or dried cranberries

$1/_4$ teaspoon ground cinnamon

1 tablespoon (15 ml) maple syrup

2 tablespoons (35 g) almond butter

Peel and dice the pear, discarding the core. Combine the diced pear, rice, rice milk, raisins, and cinnamon in a saucepan, and bring to a simmer over medium heat. Cover, reduce the heat to low, and cook 8 minutes, removing the lid to stir the porridge every few minutes. Turn off the heat and stir in the maple syrup and almond butter until well combined.

Yield: 4 servings

Each will have: 231 calories; 6 g fat; 4 g protein; 40 g carbohydrate; 3 g dietary fiber; 0 mg cholesterol.

French Toast

Every once in a while, bread will become that day-old stuff you don't know what to do with. If you have hearty breakfast eaters on hand, French toast is the answer. Serve with butter and maple syrup or your favorite jam. Fresh seasonal fruit, chopped into bite-sized pieces, also makes a wonderful topping.

Ingredients

3 large eggs

1 cup (235 ml) lowfat milk

$1/2$ teaspoon ground cinnamon

Several grinds freshly grated nutmeg

12 slices ($3/4$ inch, or 2 cm, thick) day-old crusty French bread

3 tablespoons (42 g) unsalted butter

Crack the eggs into a large glass baking dish and add the milk, cinnamon, and nutmeg. Whisk to combine. Place 3 to 4 slices of the bread in the egg mixture, pushing them down so they are completely saturated, and allow them to soak for about 1 minute.

Meanwhile, heat a cast-iron or other heavy-bottomed skillet over medium-high heat and add 1 tablespoon (14 g) butter allowing it to melt but not brown. Use a fork to transfer the bread to the skillet and cook until golden brown, about 1 minute for each side. Soak and cook the remaining bread as described above, adding more of the butter as needed. Serve immediately or wrap in foil to keep hot for several minutes before serving. Pass your favorite toppings.

Yield: 6 servings

Each will have: 242 calories; 10 g fat; 9 g protein; 28 g carbohydrate; 2 g dietary fiber; 123 mg cholesterol.

Cottage Cheese Pancakes

Serve these tasty pancakes with preserves, fresh seasonal fruit, or a drizzle of syrup.

Ingredients

3 large eggs

3 tablespoons (25 g) whole-wheat flour

$3/4$ cup (170 g) lowfat cottage cheese

3 tablespoons (45 ml) half-and-half

Pinch salt

2 tablespoons (28 g) unsalted butter

Separate the eggs, placing the whites in a small bowl and the yolks in a larger bowl. Use an electric mixer to beat the whites until stiff peaks form. Set aside. Add the flour, cottage cheese, half-and-half, and salt to the egg yolks and whisk to combine. Gently fold the egg whites into the egg yolk mixture.

Heat a cast-iron or other heavy-bottomed skillet over medium heat. Place one tablespoon of butter in the skillet, allowing it to melt but not brown. Add batter in $1/4$-cup (60 g) amounts, cooking as many pancakes at once as will fit in the pan. Cook until bubbles begin to form on the surface, about 1 or 2 minutes, then turn and cook on the other side until golden brown. Repeat with remaining batter, adding more of the butter as needed.

Yield: 4 servings

Each will have: 178 calories; 12 g fat; 12 g protein; 6 g carbohydrate; 1 g dietary fiber; 182 mg cholesterol.

Tempeh Rancheros

This delicious south-of-the-border concoction can be served for lunch or dinner as well as breakfast. Its name implies a hearty ranch-hand breakfast, and it certainly is substantial, especially when served with the traditional refried beans and/or Mexican rice.

Ingredients

1 tablespoon (15 ml) canola oil

$1/2$ yellow onion, diced

$1/2$ green bell pepper, diced

$1/2$ red bell pepper, diced

1 can (14 ounces, or 400 g) diced tomatoes, with juice

2 tablespoons (18 g) diced pickled jalapeño pepper

2 teaspoons crushed garlic

2 teaspoons pure chili powder

1 teaspoon ground cumin

$1/2$ teaspoon salt

Several grinds black pepper

12 ounces (340 g) soy tempeh, cut into $1/2$ x 3-inch (1.25 x 7.5-cm) strips

8 corn tortillas

1 cup (115 g) shredded pepper jack cheese

Heat the oil in a large sauté pan over medium-high heat. Add the onion and bell peppers and sauté, stirring frequently, for 3 minutes. Add the tomatoes, jalapeño pepper, garlic, chili powder, cumin, salt, and pepper. Stir to combine, cover, and cook 8 minutes.

Remove the lid and nestle the tempeh pieces into the sauce. Cover and cook 3 minutes. Just before serving time, wrap the tortillas in a tea towel and heat in a microwave oven until steaming hot, about 1 minute. (Alternatively, you may toast the tortillas one at a time in a hot, dry skillet or over a gas flame, turning frequently.)

Serve the tempeh in shallow bowls with a generous helping of sauce on top. Sprinkle with cheese and nestle 2 folded tortillas in each bowl.

Yield: 4 servings

Each will have: 401 calories; 16 g fat; 21 g protein; 44 g carbohydrate; 5 g dietary fiber; 3 mg cholesterol.

Southwest Potato, Tofu, and Spinach Scramble

For a hearty work-morning breakfast, a tofu-and-potato dish like this one hits the mark. Warmed corn tortillas are delicious on the side, and fresh mango or pineapple would make a perfect fruit offering at the end of the meal.

Ingredients

1 tablespoon (15 ml) extra-virgin olive oil

2 medium red potatoes, finely diced

$^1/_2$ medium yellow onion, finely diced

2 tablespoons (18 g) minced pickled jalapeño pepper

2 teaspoons pure chili powder

1 teaspoon dried oregano

1 teaspoon ground cumin

12 ounces (340 g) firm tofu, crumbled

$^1/_2$ teaspoon salt

6 ounces (170 g) prewashed baby spinach

Heat the olive oil in a heavy-bottomed skillet over medium-high heat and sauté the potatoes, onion, jalapeño, chili powder, oregano, and cumin for 3 minutes, stirring frequently.

Add the tofu and salt and stir to combine. Add $^1/_2$ cup (120 ml) water and immediately cover the pan. Cook for 5 minutes. If the pan is very dry, stir in about 2 tablespoons (28 ml) water. Mound the spinach on top of the tofu mixture, cover, and cook until the spinach wilts, about 2 minutes.

Stir to incorporate the spinach into the tofu and potatoes. If there is still some watery liquid remaining in the pan, continue to cook, uncovered, until most of it has evaporated, about 1 minute longer.

Yield: 4 servings

Each will have: 149 calories; 8 g fat; 9 g protein; 13 g carbohydrate; 3 g dietary fiber; 0 mg cholesterol.

Curried Tofu Scramble with Roasted Peppers and Peas

This is a wonderful combination of flavors. Serve it with whole-grain toast or warmed chapatis and Spiced Mango and Banana Lassi (page 211) for sipping.

Ingredients

1 tablespoon (15 ml) canola oil
1 pound (455 g) firm tofu, crumbled
$^1/_2$ medium yellow onion, finely diced
1 tablespoon curry powder
$^1/_2$ teaspoon salt
Several grinds black pepper
1 cup (130 g) frozen shelled peas
$^1/_2$ cup (90 g) chopped roasted red bell pepper
$^1/_4$ cup (15 g) fresh cilantro leaves

Heat the olive oil in a heavy-bottomed skillet over medium-high heat. Add the tofu, onion, curry powder, salt, and black pepper and sauté, for 2 minutes, stirring frequently.

Add $^1/_2$ cup (120 ml) water and immediately cover the pan. Cook for 3 minutes. Stir in the peas, roasted pepper, and cilantro; cover and cook for 2 minutes.

Yield: 4 servings

Each will have: 159 calories; 9 g fat; 11 g protein; 11 g carbohydrate; 3 g dietary fiber; 0 mg cholesterol.

Scrambled Eggs with Goat Cheese and Fresh Herbs

This is a wonderful brunch dish for two—expand it to serve more by simply multiplying the ingredients. Serve it with your favorite toast and a side of fresh summer fruit. For the fresh herbs, we like to use parsley, sage, basil, and oregano.

Ingredients

4 large eggs

1 tablespoon (15 ml) lowfat milk

$1/8$ teaspoon salt

Several grinds black pepper

$1/2$ tablespoon extra-virgin olive oil

$1/3$ cup (40 g) crumbled fresh goat cheese (chèvre)

$1/4$ cup (15 g) finely chopped mixed fresh herbs

In a bowl, whip the eggs with the milk, salt, and pepper until well blended. Heat the oil in a heavy-bottomed skillet or omelet pan over medium heat. When it is hot, add the eggs and shake the pan to distribute them evenly. Cook for 1 minute, then distribute the goat cheese and herbs over the eggs. Use a heatproof rubber spatula to gently turn and fold the eggs until they are completely cooked but soft and fluffy, not dry.

Yield: 2 servings

Each will have: 274 calories; 20 g fat; 19 g protein; 3 g carbohydrate; trace dietary fiber; 444 mg cholesterol.

Water Chestnut and Bean Sprout Omelets

This simple omelet, based on the Chinese preparation known as egg foo yung, is wonderful as a brunch or light supper entrée. Serve it sprinkled with soy sauce or with sweet Asian chili sauce, which is available at Asian markets.

Ingredients

4 green onions
5 large eggs, well beaten
$1/2$ teaspoon granulated garlic
$1/2$ teaspoon salt
Several grinds black pepper
8 ounces (225 g) mung bean sprouts, rinsed and patted dry
1 can (8 ounces, or 225 g) sliced water chestnuts, drained
2 tablespoons (28 ml) canola oil, divided

Thinly slice the green onions, discarding the root tips and some of the green portion. Crack the eggs into a medium bowl and whisk until frothy. Whisk in the granulated garlic, salt, and pepper. Stir in the bean sprouts, water chestnuts, and green onions.

Place a heavy-bottomed skillet over medium-high heat and add 1 tablespoon (15 ml) oil. Ladle about $1/4$ cup (60 g) of the egg mixture at a time into the pan to form patties. The mixture will be runny, so use a spatula to keep the edges contained as the eggs set. Cook for about 2 minutes to lightly brown one side, then turn and cook until completely set, about 1 minute longer. Place the patties on a warmed serving platter and cover with a clean kitchen towel. Add the remaining 1 tablespoon (15 ml) oil to the pan and cook the remaining egg mixture as directed above. Transfer to the platter and serve.

Yield: 4 servings
Each will have: 204 calories; 13 g fat; 10 g protein; 12 g carbohydrate; 3 g dietary fiber; 265 mg cholesterol.

Poached Eggs with Fresh Shiitake Mushroom Sauté

Invite friends over for this perfect Sunday-morning breakfast.

Ingredients

2 tablespoons (28 ml) white vinegar

4 fresh shiitake mushrooms

1 tablespoon (15 ml) extra-virgin olive oil

1 1/2 teaspoons mirin

1/2 teaspoon soy sauce

1/2 teaspoons seasoned rice vinegar

Pinch of salt

Several grinds black pepper

2 small shallots, minced

2 whole-wheat English muffins

4 large eggs

Place about 2 inches (5 cm) of water in a large, shallow sauté pan or skillet (avoid cast iron), cover, and bring to a rapid simmer over high heat. Add the white vinegar.

Meanwhile, discard the stems of the mushrooms and thinly slice the caps. Combine the olive oil, mirin, soy sauce, rice vinegar, salt, and pepper in a separate small skillet over medium heat. Add the shallots and mushrooms and sauté until the mushrooms are limp, about 3 to 4 minutes. Cut the English muffins in half and toast them.

While the mushrooms sauté, use a spoon to stir the vinegar-water in a circular motion. Carefully break the eggs into the swirling water, keeping the water moving by gently stirring. Cook over low heat until the whites are firm, about 3 to 5 minutes. You can spoon some water over the yolks to finish cooking them if they have not set.

Place half of a toasted English muffin in the center of four individual serving plates. Remove the eggs from the water with a slotted spoon, being careful not to break them. Drain for a moment before placing them on top of the muffins. Spoon the sautéed mushrooms over the top.

Yield: 4 servings

Each will have: 188 calories; 9 g fat; 10 g protein; 18 g carbohydrate; 2 g dietary fiber; 212 mg cholesterol.

Poached Eggs on a Bed of Sautéed Spinach

Spinach for breakfast? Why not? Served with a poached egg on top, the bed of spinach makes an elegant presentation.

Ingredients

2 tablespoons (28 ml) white vinegar

2 tablespoons (28 ml) extra-virgin olive oil

$^1/_2$ red onion, thinly sliced

4 cloves garlic, minced

2 tablespoons (28 ml) dry white wine

12 ounces (340 g) prewashed baby
  spinach

$^1/_8$ teaspoon salt

2 teaspoons freshly squeezed lemon juice

4 slices French bread

4 large eggs

Place about 2 inches (5 cm) of water in a large, shallow sauté pan or skillet (avoid cast iron), cover, and bring to a rapid simmer over high heat. Add the white vinegar.

Meanwhile, place the oil in a large, deep skillet or wok over medium heat and add the red onion and garlic. Sauté for about 2 minutes, stirring frequently, then add the wine. Add the spinach and salt, along with 2 tablespoons (28 ml) water. Cover the pan and steam for 4 to 5 minutes, until the spinach wilts. Remove the lid to stir occasionally. Add the lemon juice at the end of the cooking time and stir to combine. Toast the bread.

While the spinach cooks, use a spoon to stir the vinegar-water in a circular motion. Carefully break the eggs into the swirling water, keeping the water moving by gently stirring. Cook over low heat until the whites are firm, about 3 to 5 minutes. You can spoon some water over the yolks to finish cooking them if they have not set.

Remove the spinach from the pan with a slotted spoon, drain for a moment, and place equal amounts in the center of four individual serving plates. Remove the eggs from the water with a slotted spoon, being careful not to break them. Drain for a moment before placing them on top of the spinach. Serve a slice of toasted bread on each plate.

Yield: 4 servings

Each will have: 237 calories; 13 g fat; 11 g protein; 19 g carbohydrate; 3 g dietary fiber; 212 mg cholesterol.

CHAPTER FOUR

15-MINUTE APPETIZERS AND SNACKS

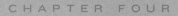

People love to nibble, and it's a pleasure to provide something besides the standard chips and supermarket dip for family and friends to enjoy. In this chapter, we present a variety of simple savory appetizers. Set them out to be enjoyed with a glass of wine or other aperitif while you finish preparing dinner.

Many of these concoctions, including all the bean spreads, can be prepared ahead of time and stored in the refrigerator for several days, providing healthy options when the snacking urge strikes.

Our yield for each recipe in this chapter assumes that no other appetizers are being served. If you are offering an assortment, assume that each recipe will serve more people.

As an easy and festive party idea, select several of these recipes (see "Fantastic Appetizer Buffet" on page 49) and serve them in your favorite bowls, platters, and baskets. Make the food earlier in the day, arrange a pretty buffet table, and enjoy mingling with your guests.

APPETIZERS ARE EVEN EASIER WHEN YOU FOLLOW THESE TIPS.

Some dips and spreads are so simple they don't need a recipe! Blend small amounts of your favorite herbs or spices, such as fresh dill or curry, with softened cream cheese, cottage cheese, yogurt, or sour cream. Add minced onion, garlic, and crunchy chopped nuts or seeds, if desired.

Most of our dips and spreads will stay fresh and tasty for up to a week if stored in a tightly closed container in the refrigerator.

Leftover dips and spreads should be refrigerated, but they taste best when served at room temperature. Set them out a couple of hours ahead of time, if possible.

Canned beans are great convenience foods for making spreads or dips. Or you can substitute $1^{1}/_{2}$ cups (265 g) home-cooked beans (see page 237 for bean-cooking instructions) for 1 can (15 ounces, or 420 g).

Look for healthy alternatives to high-fat chips and crackers, avoiding hydrogenated oils and chemical additives.

Bite-sized pieces of raw or barely cooked vegetables are healthy dippers and add welcome crunch and color to an appetizer plate.

Provençal Spiced Olives

No appetizer selection is complete without olives. These zesty morsels are a snap to prepare—and they'll disappear just as fast at your next dinner party. Use a microplane zester for the orange peel or slice off paper-thin strips with a sharp paring knife, then mince.

Ingredients

1 cup (135 g) plain green or black olives, any variety

1/2 tablespoon extra-virgin olive oil

1/2 tablespoon red or white wine vinegar

1 teaspoon finely minced orange peel (zest)

1/4 teaspoon coarsely ground black pepper

1/2 teaspoon herbes de Provence

In a serving bowl, toss the olives with the oil, vinegar, orange peel, and pepper. Lightly crush the Herbes de Provence with a mortar and pestle or your fingers. Add to the olives, stir to mix, and serve immediately or store in a tightly closed container in the refrigerator and enjoy over the course of a week or two.

Yield: 8 servings

Each will have: 27 calories; 3 g fat; trace protein; 1 g carbohydrate; 1 g dietary fiber; 0 mg cholesterol.

Fantastic Appetizer Buffet

Invite eight of your friends to join you for this casual buffet dinner. Offer wine, beer, or your favorite cocktails, and provide plenty of bread and crackers for dipping and spreading. Delight your guests at the end of the evening by serving French Roast Ice Cream Floats (page 231)—coffee and dessert all in one glass!

- Provençal Spiced Olives, page 49
- Cannellini Bean Spread with Oregano and Cumin, page 58
- Artichoke and Parmesan Spread, page 54
- Spinach and Water Chestnut Dip, page 56
- Roasted Red Bell Peppers in Spicy Marinade, page 50
- Mushrooms with Cumin and Sherry Vinegar, page 51

VEGAN

Roasted Red Bell Peppers in Spicy Marinade

This strongly spiced appetizer is based on a traditional Tunisian dish. Serve it with a bean spread, flatbread, and a bowl of spiced olives to create a great appetizer or light lunch.

Ingredients

1 jar (12 ounces, or 340 g) roasted red bell peppers, drained

$1/2$ cup (130 g) canned diced tomatoes, drained

1 tablespoon (15 ml) extra-virgin olive oil

1 tablespoon (15 ml) red wine vinegar

1 teaspoon crushed garlic

$1/4$ teaspoon salt

$1/8$ teaspoon cayenne pepper

Cut the roasted red bell peppers into thin strips. Combine them in a serving dish with the tomatoes, olive oil, red wine vinegar, garlic, salt, and cayenne. Serve immediately or set aside at room temperature for a few hours so the flavors can blend and intensify.

Yield: 6 servings

Each will have: 36 calories; 2 g fat; 1 g protein; 4 g carbohydrate; 1 g dietary fiber; 0 mg cholesterol.

VEGAN

Mushrooms with Cumin and Sherry Vinegar

Picture yourself and several friends at a public house in Barcelona, sipping a glass of red wine and enjoying a plate of tapas—appetizers, Spanish-style. This one is a classic. Serve it with thinly sliced rustic bread.

Ingredients

1 pound (455 g) small crimini or white button mushrooms

2 tablespoons (28 ml) sherry vinegar

1 tablespoon (15 ml) extra-virgin olive oil

2 cloves garlic, minced

1 teaspoon ground cumin

$^1/_4$ teaspoon salt

Several grinds black pepper

2 tablespoons minced fresh Italian parsley

Cut the mushrooms in half from stem to cap. Place the vinegar, oil, garlic, cumin, salt, and pepper in a sauté pan or skillet over medium-high heat. Add the mushrooms and stir to coat with the seasonings. Cover the pan, reduce the heat to medium, and cook 5 minutes, shaking the pan occasionally.

Remove the lid, add 2 tablespoons (28 ml) water, and stir and sauté until most of the liquid has evaporated, about 2 minutes. Transfer to a serving dish and sprinkle with the parsley. Serve hot or at room temperature.

Yield: 6 servings

Each will have: 42 calories; 3 g fat; 2 g protein; 4 g carbohydrate; 1 g dietary fiber; 0 mg cholesterol.

Sprouts and Enoki Mushrooms Wrapped in Seaweed

Purchase the roasted dried nori seaweed packaged in flat sheets for this recipe (sometimes the label says "toasted," but they're one and the same). Make sure the paper towels used to moisten the nori are barely damp—if they're too wet, the nori tends to break apart. Look for the seasoned ginger, sometimes referred to as pickled, at an Asian specialty store or well-stocked supermarket. Be sure to buy the pale pink slices, not the bright red shredded variety. This recipe takes less time to prepare than to read!

Ingredients

3 sheets roasted nori seaweed

1 medium cucumber

3 green onions

$3^1/_2$ ounces (100 g) fresh enoki mushrooms

1 tablespoon wasabi paste

16 snow pea pods

6 ounces (170 g) fresh mung bean sprouts, rinsed and patted dry

4 ounces (115 g) pea sprouts

1 ounce (28 g) sliced seasoned ginger

2 tablespoons (28 ml) soy sauce

Lay one sheet of seaweed on your work surface and place a damp paper towel on top of it. Lay another sheet of seaweed on top, cover with another damp paper towel, then the third sheet and another damp paper towel. Set aside.

Peel the cucumber and cut it in half lengthwise. Use a spoon to scoop out and discard the seeds. Slice the cucumber halves lengthwise into thin strips, then cut the strips in half crosswise. Set aside. Trim off the root ends of the green onions and some of the green tops. Thinly slice the onions lengthwise and set aside. Trim off the root ends of the enoki mushrooms. Separate the mushrooms into at least 6 bundles.

Use kitchen shears to cut the sheets of nori in half. Working with 1 half-sheet at a time, spread one sixth of the wasabi paste lengthwise down the center. Arrange one-sixth of the cucumber strips alongside the wasabi and top with equal amounts of green onions, mushrooms, snow peas, mung bean sprouts, pea sprouts, and seasoned ginger. The ingredients should be overhanging each end. Roll up into a tight bundle. Fill the remaining half-sheets of seaweed with the remaining ingredients.

Use a wet knife to cut each bundle in half crosswise, and place cut-side down on a serving platter, with the filling protruding from the tops. Place the soy sauce in a small serving dish in the center of the platter and serve, allowing diners to dip the rolls into the sauce as desired.

Yield: 6 servings
Each will have: 62 calories; trace fat; 4 g protein; 13 g carbohydrate; 2 g dietary fiber; 0 mg cholesterol.

Artichoke and Parmesan Spread

Here is a crowd-pleaser that tastes great spread on any cracker or crusty bread. A dish of olives and some fresh vegetable sticks are good choices for rounding out the appetizer course.

Ingredients

1 can (14 ounces, or 400 g) water-packed
    artichoke hearts, drained
$1/4$ cup (25 g) grated Parmesan cheese
$1/4$ cup (60 g) plain nonfat yogurt
1 tablespoon (15 g) mayonnaise
1 teaspoon crushed garlic
1 teaspoon paprika
$1/4$ teaspoon salt
$1/4$ teaspoon ground black pepper

Place the artichoke hearts in a colander, rinse briefly with cold water, and set aside to drain thoroughly. Whisk together the Parmesan, yogurt, mayonnaise, garlic, paprika, salt, and black pepper until smoothly combined. Finely chop the artichoke hearts and stir them into the Parmesan mixture. Transfer to a serving bowl and garnish with a sprinkle of paprika.

Yield: 6 servings
Each will have: 72 calories; 3 g fat; 4 g protein; 9 g carbohydrate; 4 g dietary fiber; 4 mg cholesterol.

Goat Cheese Spread with Pesto and Roasted Red Bell Pepper

This colorful spread comes together in a flash. Serve it in a ramekin with thin slices of seeded baguette.

Ingredients

4 ounces (115 g) fresh goat cheese
    (chèvre)
2 tablespoons (30 g) basil pesto
1 tablespoon (15 ml) lowfat milk
$1/8$ teaspoon salt
Several grinds black pepper
2 tablespoons (25 g) minced roasted red
    bell pepper

Place the goat cheese in a bowl and add the pesto, milk, salt, and pepper. Mix with a fork until smoothly combined. Stir in the red bell pepper, transfer to a ramekin, and serve.

Yield: 6 servings
Each will have: 54 calories; 4 g fat; 4 g protein; trace carbohydrate; 0 g dietary fiber; 9 mg cholesterol.

Pumpkin Seed Cheese Spread

Pumpkin seeds, when toasted, develop a nutty flavor that blends perfectly with the cheeses. Serve with slices of sweet baguette or crisp crackers.

Ingredients

$1/4$ cup (55 g) raw, unsalted, shelled pumpkin seeds

$1 1/2$ teaspoons cumin seeds

$1/3$ cup (85 g) lowfat ricotta cheese

$3/4$ cup (115 g) crumbled feta cheese

2 cloves garlic, minced

1 tablespoon (15 ml) freshly squeezed lime juice

$1/4$ teaspoon dried thyme

$1/4$ teaspoon pure chili powder

Place the pumpkin seeds in a heavy-bottomed skillet over medium heat. Shake the pan or stir the seeds frequently as they heat up for a few minutes. When they begin to pop, add the cumin seeds to the pan and stir constantly as the pumpkin seeds finish roasting. When almost all of them have popped and they are lightly browned, transfer them directly to a food processor. Add the ricotta cheese, feta cheese, garlic, lime juice, and thyme, and puree until fairly smooth. Transfer to a ramekin or serving bowl and dust with the chili powder.

Yield: 8 servings

Each will have: 64 calories; 4 g fat; 4 g protein; 3 g carbohydrate; trace dietary fiber; 16 mg cholesterol.

Spinach and Water Chestnut Dip

Almost everyone loves spinach dip, and this version is simple to put together. Serve it in a hollowed-out round loaf of French bread, set in the center of a large platter. Cut the removed bread into cubes and pile them on the sides of the platter. This dip is also good spread on baguette slices or crackers, or served with crisp vegetables for dipping.

Ingredients

8 ounces (225 g) frozen chopped spinach

6 whole canned water chestnuts

2 green onions

$1/2$ cup (115 g) lowfat sour cream

$1/4$ cup (60 g) lowfat mayonnaise

2 tablespoons minced fresh Italian parsley

1 teaspoon dried dill weed

$1/8$ teaspoon celery seed

$1/8$ teaspoon salt

Several grinds black pepper

Place the spinach in a colander and rinse it well with hot water to thaw. Press it with the back of a wooden spoon or squeeze with your hands to remove as much excess moisture as possible. Put the water chestnuts in a food processor and pulse to chop. Mince the onions, discarding the root tips and some of the green portion. Add the onions, spinach, sour cream, mayonnaise, parsley, dill weed, celery seed, salt, and pepper to the food processor. Pulse to combine, scraping down the sides of the bowl with a rubber spatula so all the ingredients are incorporated. Transfer to a bowl or serve in a hollowed-out loaf of bread as described above.

Yield: 10 servings

Each will have: 19 calories; 1 g fat; 1 g protein; 3 g carbohydrate; 1 g dietary fiber; 4 mg cholesterol.

Tofu Avocado Dip

Serve this spring-green dip with an assortment of fresh veggies. It's also great spread on rye crispbread or thin slices of pumpernickel.

Ingredients

1 large Haas avocado

5 ounces (140 g) firm tofu

1 tablespoon (15 ml) freshly squeezed lemon juice

1 clove garlic, minced

2 teaspoons Dijon mustard

1 teaspoon soy sauce

2 green onions

Cut the avocado in half and remove the pit (see page 240). Scoop the avocado out of the skin and place it in a blender or food processor. Break the tofu into chunks and add it to the blender, along with the lemon juice, garlic, mustard, and soy sauce. Pulse to puree and transfer to a serving bowl. Mince the onions, discarding the root tips and some of the green portion. Stir the onions into the avocado dip and serve.

Yield: 8 servings

Each will have: 58 calories; 5 g fat; 2 g protein; 3 g carbohydrate; 1 g dietary fiber; 0 mg cholesterol.

Yogurt Dip with Cucumber, Garlic, and Mint

This yummy and refreshing dip can be made with soy yogurt for a vegan version. It makes a great dip for veggie sticks or crisp crackers, and is also a nice topping for veggie burgers or pita sandwiches. It doesn't keep particularly well, so finish off any leftovers within a day or two.

Ingredients

1 cup (245 g) plain nonfat yogurt

$1/4$ cup (40 g) minced red onion

$1/4$ cup (15 g) minced fresh mint

1 clove garlic, minced

$1/2$ teaspoon salt

Several grinds black pepper

1 medium cucumber

In a bowl, stir together the yogurt, red onion, mint, garlic, salt, and pepper until well combined. Peel the cucumber and cut it in half lengthwise. Use a spoon to scrape out and discard the seeds. Grate the cucumber, stir it into the yogurt mixture, and serve.

Yield: 10 servings

Each will have: 21 calories; trace fat; 2 g protein; 3 g carbohydrate; trace dietary fiber; trace cholesterol.

Black Bean Dip

This dip has been a favorite among our family members, young and old alike, for years. Serve it with a 1-pound (455-g) bag of your favorite tortilla chips. Add diced jalapeño if you are serving it to a crowd that likes a spicy dip.

Ingredients

1 can (15 ounces, or 420 g) black beans
$1/2$ cup (115 g) lowfat sour cream
$1/2$ teaspoon pure chili powder
$1/2$ teaspoon ground cumin
$1/2$ teaspoon granulated garlic
Pinch of salt

Place the beans in a colander, rinse, and drain. Combine the beans, sour cream, chili powder, cumin, granulated garlic, and salt in a food processor. Process until smooth. Transfer to a shallow bowl and serve.

Yield: 16 servings

Each will have: 94 calories; 1 g fat; 6 g protein; 17 g carbohydrate; 4 g dietary fiber; 1 mg cholesterol.

Cannellini Bean Spread with Oregano and Cumin

Cannellini beans are white beans frequently used as an ingredient in Mediterranean-style cooking. They are sold dried or precooked in 15-ounce (420-g) cans. Serve this spread with crackers or a crusty bread.

Ingredients

1 can (15 ounces, or 420 g) cannellini beans
1 tablespoon (15 ml) extra-virgin olive oil
1 tablespoon (15 ml) freshly squeezed lemon juice
1 teaspoon dried oregano
$1/2$ teaspoon ground cumin
$1/4$ teaspoon salt
$1/8$ teaspoon cayenne pepper

Place the beans in a colander, rinse, and drain. In a food processor, combine the beans with 2 tablespoons (28 ml) water, olive oil, lemon juice, oregano, cumin, salt , and cayenne. Process until smooth. Transfer to a bowl and serve.

Yield: 12 servings

Each will have: 129 calories; 1 g fat; 8 g protein; 22 g carbohydrate; 5 g dietary fiber; 0 mg cholesterol.

Hummus with Cilantro and Pickled Jalapeño

This Mexicali version of the classic Mediterranean chickpea spread is a party pleaser. It has a vivid green color and piquant, but not too spicy, flavor. Serve it with raw veggie sticks and crispy pita or tortilla chips.

Ingredients

1 can (15 ounces, or 420 g) garbanzo beans
$1/4$ cup (55 g) raw, unsalted, shelled pumpkin seeds
1 cup (60 g) chopped fresh cilantro
2 tablespoons (28 ml) freshly squeezed lime juice
2 tablespoons (18 g) minced pickled jalapeños
1 teaspoon crushed garlic
$1/2$ teaspoon salt

Place the garbanzo beans in a colander, rinse, and drain thoroughly. In a dry skillet, toast the pumpkin seeds over medium-high heat, stirring or shaking the pan frequently, until most of them have popped. Transfer them to a blender and add the garbanzos, cilantro, lime juice, pickled jalapeños, garlic, and salt. Process until smooth. Transfer to a bowl and serve.

Yield: 8 servings

Each will have: 75 calories; 1 g fat; 3 g protein; 14 g carbohydrate; 3 g dietary fiber; 0 mg cholesterol.

White Bean, Broccoli, and Walnut Spread with Fresh Basil

We like to keep bean spreads on hand for a quick snack, to spread on bread or scoop up with raw veggies. This one takes its inspiration from Mediterranean cuisine. You may substitute another white bean if you don't have cannellinis on hand.

Ingredients

3 cups (210 g) broccoli florets

1 can (15 ounces, or 420 g) cannellini beans

$^1/_2$ cup (60 g) chopped walnuts

$^1/_4$ cup (60 ml) vegetable broth

2 tablespoons (28 ml) freshly squeezed lemon juice

1 clove garlic, minced

$^1/_2$ teaspoon salt

$^1/_4$ teaspoon ground black pepper

$^1/_2$ cup (25 g) fresh basil leaves, loosely packed

$^1/_4$ teaspoon paprika

Place a steamer tray in a saucepan and add about 2 inches (5 cm) of water. Place the broccoli on the steamer tray, cover, and bring to a boil over medium-high heat. Steam until very soft, about 7 minutes. Drain and transfer the broccoli to a blender or food processor.

Add the beans, walnuts, broth, lemon juice, garlic, salt, and pepper. Pulse until smooth. Add the basil and continue pulsing until it is well chopped and bits of green are distributed throughout the mixture. Transfer to a bowl. Sprinkle evenly with the paprika, and serve.

Yield: 12 servings

Each will have: 160 calories; 3 g fat; 10 g protein; 24 g carbohydrate; 6 g dietary fiber; trace cholesterol.

Grilled Italian-Style Garlic Bread

In this simple preparation, known in Italy as bruschetta, bread is quickly toasted over a hot fire to create the characteristic grill marks. If you do not have a grill, however, a perfectly good version can be made by broiling the bread. The hot bread is then brushed with a good, fruity olive oil and fresh minced garlic. Choose an elongated loaf rather than a dome shape.

Ingredients

6 tablespoons (90 ml) extra-virgin olive oil

4 cloves garlic, minced

1 loaf thick-crusted bread, about 1 pound (455 g), cut into ¹/₂ inch
 (1.25-cm) slices

Preheat a gas grill to medium-high. Combine the oil and garlic in a small bowl and set aside. Arrange the bread slices in a single layer directly on the grill. Grill for about 2 minutes per side, until the bread is lightly browned and crisp on the outside but still soft and chewy on the inside. (Do not dry out the bread by grilling too long.) Remove from the grill and brush one side liberally with the oil and garlic mixture. Place in a serving basket or on a platter.

Yield: 12 servings

Each will have: 165 calories; 8 g fat; 3 g protein; 20 g carbohydrate; 1 g dietary fiber; 0 mg cholesterol.

Black Bean and Corn Salsa with Serrano Chiles and Lime Juice

If time permits and you're making this during the summer months, use corn freshly cut from the cob—you will need about 2 large ears. The crunch of fresh corn kernels is especially scrumptious. Serve this colorful salsa with tortilla chips. This makes enough for a large gathering. Leftover salsa can be kept in the refrigerator for 4 to 5 days.

Ingredients

1 can (15 ounces, or 420 g) black beans

1 cup (155 g) fresh or frozen corn kernels

$1/2$ medium red bell pepper, diced

1 serrano chile, seeded and minced

2 tablespoons (28 ml) freshly squeezed lime juice

2 teaspoons extra-virgin olive oil

$1/2$ teaspoon granulated garlic

$1/2$ teaspoon pure chili powder

$1/4$ teaspoon ground cumin

Place the beans in a colander, rinse, and drain. If using frozen corn, defrost in a microwave oven and pat dry, or place in a colander and rinse well with hot water to thaw. Drain well. In a medium bowl, combine the beans, corn, red bell pepper, and serrano chile. In a small bowl, whisk together the lime juice, olive oil, garlic, chili powder, and cumin. Pour over the bean mixture and toss to combine.

Yield: 10 servings

Each will have: 61 calories; 1 g fat; 3 g protein; 10 g carbohydrate; 3 g dietary fiber; 0 mg cholesterol.

VEGAN

Spicy Toasted Pumpkin Seeds

Pumpkin seeds (also called pepitas) are a popular ingredient in Mexican cooking. They make a finger-licking snack.

Ingredients

1 tablespoon (15 ml) canola oil

1/2 teaspoon ground cumin

1/2 teaspoon pure chili powder

1/4 teaspoon granulated garlic

2 cups (450 g) raw, unsalted, shelled
    pumpkin seeds

Heat the oil in a large heavy-bottomed skillet over medium heat. Add the cumin, chili powder, and garlic. Heat through for about a minute, stirring frequently to prevent scorching. Add the pumpkin seeds and stir to coat them with the spices. When the seeds begin to pop, stir or shake the pan constantly until they have all popped and turned golden brown, about 8 to 10 minutes. Serve warm or at room temperature.

Yield: 12 servings

Each will have: 61 calories; 3 g fat; 2 g protein; 6 g carbohydrate; trace dietary fiber; 0 mg cholesterol.

Dried Apricots Stuffed with Cream Cheese and Walnuts

These yummy little morsels are a big hit at parties, adding a festive note to any appetizer or dessert buffet. Dried figs also are delicious prepared this way, but you will have to remove their stems and slice each one in half before adding the cheese and walnuts.

Ingredients

1/3 cup (70 g) whipped lowfat cream
    cheese

1 tablespoon (20 g) honey

24 dried apricot halves

24 raw walnut halves

Scant 1/8 teaspoon ground nutmeg

Place the cream cheese in a small bowl, add the honey, and use a rubber spatula to blend well. Top each apricot half with a dollop of cream cheese, then top with a walnut half and arrange on a platter. Dust with the nutmeg and serve.

Yield: 8 servings

Each will have: 104 calories; 7 g fat; 3 g protein; 10 g carbohydrate; 1 g dietary fiber; 8 mg cholesterol.

CHAPTER FIVE

15-MINUTE SALADS

Ahhh, salads! Whether leafy or chunky, casually tossed together or carefully composed—countless combinations of vegetables, grains, beans, and herbs become superb salads when paired with well-made dressings.

All the salads in this chapter can be served as soon as they're prepared. Most nonleafy salads, such as Broccoli and White Bean Salad with Chutney Dressing (page 80) or Zucchini and Mushrooms in Spicy Lime Marinade (page 76), could also be made ahead and enjoyed over the course of a few days. Store them in the refrigerator, but bring them to room temperature before serving to unlock their flavors.

Our leafy salads are designed to launch or finish a multicourse feast. The chunkier salads can stand alone as warm-weather entrées. A perfect summer meal might consist of two or three different salads served with a baguette and a glass of wine.

If you have always considered the salad course to be rather bland and boring, perhaps you haven't considered the creative possibilities. We hope the diversity of recipes in this chapter will fire your enthusiasm and make you a look forward to your daily salad!

POINTERS FROM THE PROS

FOR THE FRESHEST, MOST FLAVORFUL SALADS,
USE THESE TRIED-AND-TRUE TIPS.

For the ultimate convenience, purchase pre-washed baby spinach and other salad greens in cellophane bags. Simply snip the bag open and use as needed. Check the "sell by" date on the package, and be sure to use them soon after purchase.

~~~

When you buy head lettuce, rinse it well, shake it dry, and wrap it in paper towels, then store it in a plastic bag in the crisper drawer of your refrigerator. This way, it will be ready to use at a moment's notice.

~~~

When making leafy salads, dry the greens well to avoid diluting your dressing with excess water. A salad spinner does this job superbly.

~~~

During the summer months, store several salad plates in the refrigerator. Serve composed or leafy salads on the chilled plates to keep them crisp and cool throughout the meal.

Don't drown your salads. Toss your chosen ingredients with just enough dressing to lightly coat them.

~~~

Extra-virgin olive oil, the best you can afford, is a great choice for homemade salad dressings. Likewise, excellent vinegars will produce superior results.

~~~

Serve leafy salads on small individual plates so they don't take up too much space on the dinner plate. Dense vegetable or bean salads can be served directly from the bowl they're tossed in.

~~~

When adding dressing to a salad, drizzle it evenly over the contents of the bowl so it distributes well when lightly tossed.

Butter Lettuce, Fennel, and Persimmon Salad with Sherry Vinaigrette

Use the Fuyu variety of *persimmon* for this salad. It has a bright orange color, a flat—rather than acorn—shape, and is eaten while still firm.

Ingredients

$1/4$ cup (60 ml) extra-virgin olive oil

2 tablespoons (28 ml) sherry vinegar

$1/2$ teaspoon granulated sugar

$1/4$ teaspoon crushed garlic

Several grinds black pepper

6 cups (120 g) torn butter lettuce, loosely packed

2 Fuyu persimmons, peeled and sliced

1 cup (110 g) chopped fresh fennel bulb

$1/4$ cup (30 g) crumbled fresh goat cheese (chevre)

Place the olive oil, sherry vinegar, sugar, garlic, and pepper in a small bowl and whisk until emulsified, about 1 minute. Set aside. Put the lettuce, persimmons, and fennel in a large bowl. Drizzle the dressing over the salad and toss to combine. Sprinkle on the chevre and toss again. Transfer to individual salad plates and serve.

Yield: 4 servings

Each will have: 188 calories; 16 g fat; 4 g protein; 9 g carbohydrate; 2 g dietary fiber; 7 mg cholesterol.

The Well-Dressed Salad

In addition to the dressings included with the salad recipes in this chapter, we provide a few others elsewhere in the book. They can be tossed with anything from iceberg lettuce to hand-picked baby greens from your garden.

- Red Wine Vinaigrette, page 18
- Meyer Lemon Vinaigrette, page 19
- Raspberry Vinaigrette, page 19
- Blue Cheese Dressing, page 20
- Tomato Basil Vinaigrette, page 20

Beets and Arugula with Dried Cranberries

Here is a perfect autumn salad, combining the earthy sweetness of beets with the tang of cranberries and bitterness of arugula. Baby arugula is widely available in prewashed bags; if you find large arugula leaves, simply tear them into bite-sized pieces. This salad is delicious and very pleasing to the eye.

Ingredients

$1/4$ cup (40 g) dried cranberries

2 tablespoons (28 ml) extra-virgin olive oil

2 tablespoons (28 ml) balsamic vinegar

1 teaspoon granulated sugar

$1/4$ teaspoon salt

$1/8$ teaspoon coarsely ground black pepper

8 cups (160 g) prewashed baby arugula leaves, loosely packed

1 can (8 ounces, 225 g) sliced beets, drained

In a small bowl, combine the cranberries with $1/4$ cup (60 ml) water. Microwave for 1 minute, then set aside to plump. Combine the oil, vinegar, sugar, salt, and pepper in a small bowl and whisk until emulsified, about 1 minute. In a large bowl, toss the arugula with half the dressing and arrange portions on 4 individual salad plates.

Cut the beet slices into matchsticks and mound some on each bed of arugula. Drizzle the remaining dressing over the beets. Drain the cranberries, distribute them among the salads, and serve.

Yield: 4 servings

Each will have: 93 calories; 7 g fat; 2 g protein; 7 g carbohydrate; 2 g dietary fiber; 0 mg cholesterol.

Spinach Salad with Raspberries and Walnuts

This salad is lovely to serve around the holiday season, with the bright green spinach and red raspberries. You may use a store-bought raspberry vinaigrette, or see page 19 for a quick and simple homemade version.

Ingredients

8 cups (160 g) prewashed baby spinach leaves, loosely packed

1 cup (110 g) fresh raspberries

$1/2$ cup (60 g) chopped walnuts

$1/4$ cup (40 g) diced red onion

$1/4$ cup (60 ml) Raspberry Vinaigrette (see recipe, page 19)

$1/4$ cup (30 g) crumbled feta cheese

Place the spinach, raspberries, walnuts, and onion in a large bowl. Drizzle the dressing over the salad and toss to combine. Sprinkle on the feta cheese and toss again. Transfer to individual salad plates and serve.

Yield: 4 servings

Each will have: 216 calories; 19 g fat; 6 g protein; 8 g carbohydrate; 4 g dietary fiber; 8 mg cholesterol.

Mixed Greens with Pear, Blue Cheese, and Pecans

This is a perfect wintertime salad, when D'Anjou pears—a firm, brown-skinned variety—are in season. They are the perfect complement to pungent blue cheese. You may use a store bought red wine vinaigrette, or see page 18 for a quick and simple homemade version.

Ingredients

8 cups (160 g) prewashed mixed salad greens, loosely packed

1 D'Anjou pear, cored, peeled, and thinly sliced

$1/2$ cup (60 g) crumbled blue cheese

$1/4$ cup (30 g) chopped pecans

$1/4$ cup (60 ml) red wine vinaigrette

Place the greens in a large bowl. Add the pear slices and blue cheese, and toss gently to combine. Sprinkle on the nuts and drizzle the vinaigrette over the salad. Toss to combine. Transfer to individual salad plates and serve.

Yield: 4 servings

Each will have: 212 calories; 19 g fat; 5 g protein; 6 g carbohydrate; 3 g dietary fiber; 11 mg cholesterol.

Romaine and Radish Salad with Orange Anise Vinaigrette

This salad is crisp and refreshing, as well as colorful. Enjoy it any time of year, paired with a Mexican-inspired entrée.

Ingredients

$1/8$ teaspoon anise seeds

2 tablespoons (28 ml) freshly squeezed orange juice

1 tablespoon (15 ml) extra-virgin olive oil

$1/8$ teaspoon ground cumin

$1/8$ teaspoon salt

6 cups (120 g) torn romaine lettuce, loosely packed

6 large radishes, thinly sliced

Use a mortar and pestle to crush the anise seeds. In a small bowl, whisk together the orange juice, olive oil, anise seeds, cumin, and salt until emulsified, about 1 minute. In a large bowl, combine the lettuce with the radishes. Drizzle the vinaigrette over the salad and toss to combine. Transfer to individual salad plates and serve.

Yield: 4 servings
Each will have: 47 calories; 4 g fat; 1 g protein; 3 g carbohydrate; 2 g dietary fiber; 0 mg cholesterol.

Fennel and Radicchio Salad with Balsamic Vinaigrette

Here, the licorice-like flavor of the fennel is complemented by the bitterness of radicchio, and the olive oil and balsamic vinegar bring the flavors together. The ingredients for this salad make it a cool-weather favorite.

Ingredients

2 tablespoons (28 ml) extra-virgin olive oil

1 tablespoon (15 ml) balsamic vinegar

$1/8$ teaspoon salt

Several grinds pepper

$1^1/2$ cups (165 g) chopped fresh fennel bulb

2 cups (80 g) torn radicchio, loosely packed

4 large butter lettuce leaves

In a small bowl, whisk together the olive oil, balsamic vinegar, salt, and pepper until emulsified, about 1 minute. Place the fennel and radicchio in a bowl and toss with the dressing. Arrange a lettuce leaf on each individual salad plate, mound equal portions of the fennel and radicchio on top, and serve.

Yield: 4 servings
Each will have: 99 calories; 7 g fat; 2 g protein; 8 g carbohydrate; 2 g dietary fiber; 0 mg cholesterol.

Napa Cabbage and Avocado Salad

This salad has a decidedly Asian flavor. Serve it with Tempeh Stir-Fry with Ginger and Lemon (page 130) for a lovely meal. Sunflower sprouts are available in many natural food markets. You may substitute mung bean sprouts, if you wish.

Ingredients

8 cups thinly sliced Napa cabbage, loosely packed

2 green onions

1 fresh jalapeño pepper

1 cup (100 g) sunflower sprouts, chopped

2 tablespoons (28 ml) soy sauce

1 tablespoon (15 ml) extra-virgin olive oil

1 teaspoon honey

1/2 teaspoon dark sesame oil

1/8 teaspoon ground ginger

1/8 teaspoon pure chili powder

Pinch of salt

Several grinds black pepper

1 medium Haas avocado, diced (see page 240)

Place the cabbage in a large bowl. Mince the green onions, discarding the root tips and some of the green portion. Remove the stem of the jalapeño and cut it in half lengthwise. Use a spoon to scrape out and discard the seeds, then finely mince the jalapeño. Add the green onions, sprouts, and jalapeño to the cabbage, and toss to combine.

In a small bowl, whisk together the soy sauce, olive oil, honey, sesame oil, ginger, chili powder, salt, and pepper until emulsified, about 1 minute. Pour over the cabbage mixture and toss to coat. Add the avocado and toss gently to combine.

Yield: 8 servings

Each will have: 68 calories; 6 g fat; 1 g protein; 4 g carbohydrate; 1 g dietary fiber; 0 mg cholesterol.

Carrot Salad with Cilantro and Lemon

The freshly squeezed lemon juice is a nice counterpoint to the natural sweetness of the carrot. Cilantro lends its signature flavor to the salad but does not overpower it. This salad could be made ahead and chilled until serving time.

Ingredients

1 large carrot

2 green onions

2 tablespoons minced fresh cilantro

1 tablespoon (15 ml) freshly squeezed
   lemon juice

$1/8$ teaspoon salt

Pinch of cayenne

Scrub the carrot clean and grate it. Mince the green onions, discarding the root tips and some of the green portion. Place the grated carrot in a bowl, along with the green onions, cilantro, lemon juice, and salt. Toss to combine. Sprinkle with the cayenne and serve.

Yield: 2 servings

Each will have: 22 calories; trace fat; 1 g protein; 5 g carbohydrate; 2 g dietary fiber; 0 mg cholesterol.

Tomatoes with Shallots and Fresh Basil

This very simple salad is a classic summer side dish. Use about 2 large, perfectly ripe red or yellow tomatoes. Serve it with your favorite pasta or a grilled entrée. It's a beautiful presentation!

Ingredients

1 pound (455 g) tomatoes

$1/4$ teaspoon salt

Several grinds black pepper

$1/2$ tablespoon extra-virgin olive oil

$1/2$ tablespoon red wine vinegar

1 medium shallot, minced

4 or 5 large fresh basil leaves, torn

Slice the tomatoes $1/4$-inch (6.25-mm) thick and fan the slices out on a platter. Sprinkle evenly with the salt and pepper. Drizzle the olive oil and vinegar evenly over the tomatoes, then top with the shallot and basil and serve.

Yield: 4 servings

Each will have: 39 calories; 2 g fat; 1 g protein; 5 g carbohydrate; 1 g dietary fiber; 0 mg cholesterol.

Cherry Tomato Salad with Green Onions and Cilantro

The colors and flavors combined in this recipe are lively, bright, and satisfying. Serve it with any Mexican or Southwest inspired entrée.

Ingredients

1 pound (455 g) cherry tomatoes

6 green onions

2 teaspoons pure chili powder

2 teaspoons dried oregano

$1/2$ teaspoon crushed garlic

$1/8$ teaspoon salt

Several grinds black pepper

2 tablespoons (28 ml) freshly squeezed lime juice

2 tablespoons (28 ml) apple cider vinegar

6 cups (120 g) torn butter lettuce, loosely packed

$1/4$ cup (15 g) minced fresh cilantro

Wash the tomatoes, pat them dry, and cut them in half. Place them in a large bowl. Mince the green onions, discarding the root tips and some of the green portion. Add them to the tomatoes, along with the chili powder, oregano, garlic, salt, and pepper. Drizzle with the lime juice and vinegar. Add the lettuce and cilantro and toss to combine. Transfer to individual salad plates and serve.

Yield: 6 servings
Each will have: 33 calories; 1 g fat; 2 g protein; 7 g carbohydrate; 2 g dietary fiber; 0 mg cholesterol.

VEGAN

Green Bean Salad with Asian Flavors

This is a wonderful way to enjoy summer's bounty of green beans. This dish is great served immediately, while it's still warm, but it also can be made ahead and left to marinate in the refrigerator for a day or two before serving.

Ingredients

1 pound (455 g) fresh green beans

2 tablespoons (28 ml) unseasoned rice vinegar

1 tablespoon (15 ml) extra-virgin olive oil

1 tablespoon (15 ml) mirin or dry sherry

2 teaspoons soy sauce

1 teaspoon dark sesame oil

1 clove garlic, minced

$1/4$ teaspoon coarsely ground black pepper

1 teaspoon sesame seeds

Place a steamer tray in a large saucepan, pour about 2 inches (5 cm) of water into the pan, and bring to a boil over medium-high heat. Cut off and discard the stem ends of the beans and remove the strings, if necessary. Leave the beans whole. Place them in the steamer tray and cover the pan. Steam until fork-tender, about 8 minutes.

Meanwhile, whisk together the vinegar, olive oil, mirin, soy sauce, sesame oil, garlic, and pepper until emulsified, about 1 minute. Set aside.

Toast the sesame seeds in a small, dry pan over medium heat, stirring them continually until they turn a darker shade of tan and emit a toasted aroma, about 1 minute. Immediately remove them from the pan and set aside.

When the beans are fork-tender, rinse them briefly with cold water and drain very well. Toss the warm beans with the dressing in a serving dish. Sprinkle with the sesame seeds and serve.

Yield: 4 servings

Each will have: 84 calories; 5 g fat; 2 g protein; 8 g carbohydrate; 4 g dietary fiber; 0 mg cholesterol.

Nopalito Salad with Pickled Jalapeños

Nopales—prickly pear cactus pads—are available fresh year-round in Mexican specialty markets and some large supermarkets, but they do require laborious preparation. This recipe calls for sliced nopales that are sold in a jar, ready to use. Look for them in a supermarket or any Mexican specialty market. If you can't find *queso fresco*—fresh Mexican cheese—you may substitute a mild feta.

Ingredients

2 cups (300 g) jarred sliced *nopales* cactus,
  drained and chopped into 2-inch (5-cm) pieces
$1/2$ cup (30 g) minced fresh Italian parsley
$1/4$ cup (40 g) minced red onion
2 tablespoons (28 ml) extra-virgin olive oil
1 tablespoon (9 g) minced pickled jalapeño
1 tablespoon (15 ml) freshly squeezed lime juice
4 large butter lettuce leaves
1 large tomato, sliced
$1/2$ cup (75 g) crumbled *queso fresco*

Place the nopales in a large bowl and add the parsley, onion, olive oil, pickled jalapeño, and lime juice. Toss to combine. Arrange a lettuce leaf on each individual salad plate and top with a portion of the nopales. Arrange the tomato slices around the edge of each plate, sprinkle with queso fresco, and serve.

Yield: 4 servings
Each will have: 116 calories; 8 g fat; 2 g protein; 8 g carbohydrate; 1 g dietary fiber; 5 mg cholesterol.

VEGAN

Zucchini and Mushrooms in Spicy Lime Marinade

Enjoy this salad often during the summer, when zucchini is abundant and cool vegetables are most appetizing. It is best to use medium-size zucchini, rather than large ones that have well-developed seed pockets. Any leftovers can be refrigerated and enjoyed over the course of a day or two.

Ingredients

1 pound (455 g) zucchini

$1/4$ cup (60 ml) freshly squeezed lime juice

2 tablespoons (28 ml) extra-virgin olive oil

2 teaspoons pure chili powder

1 teaspoon crushed garlic

$1/2$ teaspoon ground cumin

$1/2$ teaspoon salt

Several grinds black pepper

8 ounces (225 g) sliced button mushrooms

$1/2$ white onion, diced

$1/4$ cup (15 g) minced fresh cilantro

Place a steamer tray in a large saucepan, pour about 2 inches (5 cm) of water into the pan, and put on to boil over medium-high heat. Trim off and discard the ends of the zucchini. Slice each zucchini in half lengthwise, then cut the halves crosswise into $1/2$-inch (1.25-cm) slices. Place zucchini in the steamer tray, cover, and steam for 4 to 6 minutes, until tender-crisp. Rinse with cold water and drain in a colander. Pat dry with a paper towel.

Meanwhile, in a small bowl, whisk together the lime juice, olive oil, chili powder, garlic, cumin, salt, and pepper until emulsified, about 1 minute. Place the mushrooms in a large bowl, add the onion and zucchini, and toss. Drizzle the dressing over the vegetables, sprinkle on the cilantro, and toss to combine.

Yield: 8 servings

Each will have: 52 calories; 4 g fat; 1 g protein; 5 g carbohydrate; 1 g dietary fiber; 0 mg cholesterol.

Mushroom, Radish, and Celery Salad with Lemon and Garlic

These ingredients are available year-round, so serve this colorful salad frequently.

Ingredients

2 tablespoons (28 ml) freshly squeezed lemon juice

1 tablespoon (15 ml) extra-virgin olive oil

$1/4$ teaspoon crushed garlic

$1/4$ teaspoon salt

Several grinds black pepper

$1/4$ cup (15 g) minced fresh Italian parsley

8 ounces (225 g) sliced button mushrooms

1 cup (100 g) thinly sliced red radishes

1 cup (100 g) thinly sliced celery hearts

4 large butter lettuce leaves

Whisk together the lemon juice, olive oil, garlic, salt, and pepper until emulsified, about 1 minute. Stir in the parsley. Combine the mushrooms, radishes, and celery in a bowl, and pour the dressing over them. Toss to combine. Arrange a lettuce leaf on each individual salad plate and mound a portion of the mushroom mixture on each.

Yield: 4 servings

Each will have: 65 calories; 4 g fat; 2 g protein; 7 g carbohydrate; 2 g dietary fiber; 0 mg cholesterol.

Cucumber and Garlic Salad

In Greece, this simple salad—known as tzatziki—is frequently served. Enjoy it as a refreshing salad on a hot summer day. Serve plain or atop a butter lettuce leaf.

Ingredients

1 English cucumber

$1/2$ cup (125 g) plain nonfat yogurt

2 small cloves garlic, minced

1 teaspoon white wine

$1/8$ teaspoon salt

Several grinds black pepper

4 large butter lettuce leaves

Peel the cucumber and cut it in half lengthwise. Use a spoon to scrape out and discard the seeds. Cut the cucumber halves crosswise into $1/4$-inch (6.25-mm) slices. Place the slices on paper towels to blot dry.

Meanwhile, in a small bowl, whisk together the yogurt, garlic, white wine, salt, and pepper. Place the cucumber in a bowl, add the dressing, and toss gently.

Yield: 4 servings

Each will have: 30 calories; trace fat; 3 g protein; 5 g carbohydrate; 1 g dietary fiber; 1 mg cholesterol.

Red Cabbage, Green Soybeans, and Carrots with Blue Cheese Dressing

This salad offers a punch of vivid color, along with great texture and flavor. We used a mandoline to cut the cabbage into paper-thin shreds. Look for "shredded" carrots—matchstick sized pieces—in the produce section of your market. Use a store-bought blue cheese dressing, or make your own (page 20).

Ingredients

2 green onions
2 cups (140 g) finely shredded red cabbage, firmly packed
1 cup (255 g) shelled fresh green soybeans (edamame)
1 cup (120 g) shredded carrots
$1/8$ teaspoon salt
Several grinds black pepper
$1/2$ cup (125 g) blue cheese dressing

Thinly slice the green onions, discarding the root tips and most of the green portion. In a large bowl, combine the cabbage with the soybeans, carrots, and green onion. Sprinkle with the salt and pepper and toss to combine, then add the blue cheese dressing and toss again until it is well distributed.

Yield: 4 servings
Each will have: 273 calories; 21 g fat; 11 g protein; 15 g carbohydrate; 4 g dietary fiber; 18 mg cholesterol.

Green Pea and Celery Salad

This salad is the perfect side dish to include in a springtime buffet. The bright green peas and the crisp celery make a tasty combination. Feel free to make the salad a day ahead of time, but add the cashews right before serving so they don't get soggy.

Ingredients

2 cups (300 g) frozen shelled peas
1 cup (120 g) finely diced celery
$1/2$ cup (65 g) chopped salted cashews
$1/4$ cup (40 g) minced red onion
$1/4$ cup (60 g) lowfat sour cream
$1/4$ teaspoon crushed garlic

Place the frozen peas in a colander and run hot water over them for a minute or so, until thoroughly defrosted. Drain well and place on paper towels; blot dry.

Put the peas in a large bowl, along with the celery, cashews, and red onion. Toss to combine. In a small bowl, whisk together the sour cream and garlic. Pour this over the pea mixture and toss to coat.

Yield: 8 servings
Each will have: 84 calories; 4 g fat; 4 g protein; 9 g carbohydrate; 2 g dietary fiber; 1 mg cholesterol.

VEGAN

Rice, Red Pepper, and Bean Sprouts with Ginger-Peanut Dressing

This is a delicious main dish salad, perfect for a patio lunch on a hot day. Crisp rice crackers and iced green tea would be perfect accompaniments.

Ingredients

$1/4$ cup (65 g) creamy peanut butter

2 tablespoons (28 ml) apple cider vinegar

1 tablespoon (15 ml) soy sauce

2 teaspoons grated fresh ginger

1 teaspoon granulated sugar

$1/8$ teaspoon cayenne pepper

3 green onions

2 cups (390 g) cooked brown rice, cold

1 cup (120 g) shredded carrots

1 small red bell pepper, finely diced

4 large red lettuce leaves

1 cup (105 g) mung bean sprouts, rinsed and patted dry

Place the peanut butter in a bowl and whisk in $1/3$ cup (80 ml) cold water. Add the vinegar, soy sauce, ginger, sugar, and cayenne and whisk until smooth.

Thinly slice the green onions, discarding the root tips and some of the green portion. In a large bowl, toss the rice with the carrot, bell pepper, green onions, and peanut dressing until well distributed. Arrange a lettuce leaf on each individual salad plate. Mound a portion of the salad on each leaf, then garnish with a portion of the bean sprouts.

Yield: 4 servings

Each will have: 256 calories; 9 g fat; 9 g protein; 37 g carbohydrate; 6 g dietary fiber; 0 mg cholesterol.

Broccoli and White Bean Salad with Chutney Dressing

This recipe makes a wonderful dinner-party dish for eight. However, you can prepare it for fewer diners and store the leftovers in the refrigerator to be enjoyed over the next few days.

Ingredients

2 cups (140 g) fresh bite-size broccoli florets

$2/3$ cup (160 g) plain nonfat yogurt

$1/4$ cup (65 g) mango chutney

1 teaspoon curry powder

1 can (15 ounces, or 420 g) cannellini beans

$1/3$ cup (40 g) slivered almonds

8 butter lettuce leaves

3 tablespoons (12 g) minced chives

Place a steamer tray in a saucepan, pour about 2 inches (5 cm) of water into the pan, and put on to boil over medium-high heat. Place the broccoli on the steamer tray, cover the pan, and cook until barely fork-tender, about 5 minutes. Transfer the broccoli to a colander, rinse with cold water to stop the cooking, and drain well.

Meanwhile, place the yogurt in a small bowl and whisk in the chutney and curry powder. Set aside. Drain the beans into a colander and rinse. Pat them dry with a paper towel. Transfer the broccoli to a large bowl and add the beans and almonds. Pour in the yogurt dressing and toss to combine. Line eight salad bowls with the butter lettuce leaves and mound the broccoli mixture on top. Garnish with the chives.

Yield: 8 servings

Each will have: 251 calories; 4 g fat; 16 g protein; 41 g carbohydrate; 9 g dietary fiber; trace cholesterol.

VEGAN

Garbanzo Bean and Zucchini Salad with Roasted Red Peppers and Mustard Vinaigrette

This Spanish-style bean salad is hearty yet refreshing. Serve it on a bed of greens for a wonderful summer lunch, along with Quick and Classic Gazpacho (page 86) and breadsticks.

Ingredients

1 can (15 ounces, or 420 g) garbanzo beans

2 tablespoons (28 ml) freshly squeezed lemon juice

1 tablespoon (15 ml) extra-virgin olive oil

1 tablespoon (15 g) Dijon mustard

1 tablespoon (16 g) tomato paste

1 teaspoon crushed garlic

1 tablespoon capers (9 g), drained and chopped

$1/8$ teaspoon salt

$1/4$ teaspoon ground black pepper

2 medium zucchini, finely diced

1 cup (180 g) coarsely chopped roasted red bell pepper

Place the beans in a colander, rinse briefly with cold water, and set aside to drain. In a large bowl, whisk together the lemon juice, oil, mustard, tomato paste, garlic, capers, salt, and pepper until emulsified, about 1 minute. Add the beans, zucchini, and bell pepper to the bowl and toss to combine.

Yield: 6 servings

Each will have: 124 calories; 3 g fat; 5 g protein; 20 g carbohydrate; 5 g dietary fiber; 0 mg cholesterol.

CHAPTER SIX

15-MINUTE SOUPS AND STEWS

Most people think great soups require long hours of simmering on the stove. Not so! This chapter showcases innovative combinations of ingredients and seasonings that create satisfying soups and stews in a flash. We also include our quick takes on some classic soups from around the world.

A hot and hearty soup or stew, such as Tex-Mex Black Bean and Pumpkin Soup (page 97), can be the focus of attention at a rustic meal, accompanied by bread or rolls and a green salad. On the other hand, a lighter offering, such as Bread and Garlic Soup (page 87), can be served as an inviting first course. A cold soup, such as Quick and Classic Gazpacho (page 86) or Chilled Avocado and Fresh Basil Soup (page 85), is a very refreshing way to begin a summer meal.

If your quick soup repertoire is limited to canned and dried varieties, this chapter will open your eyes to an abundance of diverse and delicious new possibilities.

POINTERS FROM THE PROS

TRY THESE TIPS FOR SUPERB SOUPS AND STEWS.

Acquire a heavy pot of at least a 4-quart capacity, with a tight-fitting lid. It will serve you well for many purposes in addition to soup making, such as steaming vegetables.

Heating broth in the microwave before using it in a recipe can shave several minutes from soup preparation time.

Any of our lighter, brothy soups are great for pairing with the sandwiches or salads found elsewhere in this book.

Leftover soup can be stored in a covered container in the refrigerator for a few days. Some soups even improve in the process! Reheat them in the microwave or over a gentle flame to avoid scorching.

Frequently used seasonings and condiments—such as basil pesto, mayonnaise, and curry powder—are available in all major supermarkets, but they are simple and economical to make at home and keep on hand. See Chapter 2, "Seasonings, Condiments, and Simple Sauces" (page 16), for these useful recipes.

You can easily cook beans, grains, and vegetable stock from scratch. See "Preparing Frequently Used Ingredients" on page 234 to learn how.

To prevent scorched taste buds, allow soup to cool slightly before serving.

Chilled Avocado and Fresh Basil Soup

This velvety soup makes a wonderful first course at an al fresco dinner party. Serve it in small portions, perhaps in pretty dessert dishes or champagne glasses. It can be made up to a few hours ahead of serving time. If made ahead, set it aside in the refrigerator and serve chilled.

Ingredients

2 large Haas avocados

1 cup (245 g) plain nonfat yogurt

$^1/_2$ cup (120 g) canned diced tomatoes, undrained

1 tablespoon (15 ml) freshly squeezed lemon juice

$^1/_2$ cup (20 g) fresh basil leaves, loosely packed

$^1/_2$ teaspoon salt

$^1/_8$ teaspoon cayenne pepper

Whole basil leaves for garnish (optional)

Cut the avocados in half and remove the pits (see page 240). Scoop the avocado out of the skin and place it in a blender or food processor. Add the yogurt, tomatoes, lemon juice, basil leaves, salt, and cayenne and puree until smooth. Ladle into individual dishes and garnish each serving with a whole basil leaf.

Yield: 4 servings

Each will have: 203 calories; 16 g fat; 6 g protein; 14 g carbohydrate; 3 g dietary fiber; 1 mg cholesterol.

Broth: The Soul of Good Soup

Nothing contributes more to the flavor of homemade soups than a good broth. For the best quality, learn to make your own, using our recipe on page 239. It's a great way to use vegetable trimmings and bottom-drawer remnants, rather than relegating them to the compost heap. Making broth is a simple and homey task that fills the house with savory aromas.

Of course, there are other options. Good dried vegetable-broth powders are available either in bulk or in boxes at natural food stores. They are generally lower in sodium and other additives than those ubiquitous foil-wrapped broth cubes sold in supermarkets, and are worth seeking out. Canned broths also often include unwanted ingredients. However, the liquid broth that is typically sold in quart-size waxed cartons can be a good choice, since many brands cater to the health-conscious consumer.

Quick and Classic Gazpacho

Served on a summer afternoon as lunch or a refreshing snack, chilled gazpacho is a delicious strategy for cooling off. Increase the "zip," if you wish, by using more jalapeño pepper. Serve immediately, or chill up to a few hours before serving. You may garnish each serving with a dollop of sour cream or some diced avocado, if you wish.

Ingredients

1 medium cucumber

1 cup (240 g) canned diced tomatoes, undrained

$^1/_2$ cup (80 g) finely diced red onion

$^1/_2$ cup (90 g) finely diced roasted red bell pepper

1 cup (235 ml) low-sodium tomato-vegetable juice blend (such as V8)

2 tablespoons (28 ml) red wine vinegar

2 tablespoons (28 ml) extra-virgin olive oil

2 teaspoons minced pickled jalapeño pepper

1 clove garlic, coarsely chopped

$^1/_2$ teaspoon salt

2 tablespoons (8 g) minced fresh Italian parsley

Peel the cucumber and cut it in half lengthwise. With a spoon, scrape out and discard the seeds. Dice the cucumber very finely and place it in a large bowl. Add half the tomatoes, half the onion, and half the roasted pepper and set aside.

In a blender or food processor, combine the remaining canned tomatoes, onion, and roasted pepper with the juice, vinegar, olive oil, jalapeño, garlic, and salt. Puree and add to the bowl containing the cucumber. Add the parsley. Stir to combine.

Yield: 4 servings

Each will have: 107 calories; 7 g fat; 2 g protein; 11 g carbohydrate; 2 g dietary fiber; 0 mg cholesterol.

VEGAN

Bread and Garlic Soup

Do you ever wonder what to do with stale crusty bread? Pane cotto—Italian bread soup—is the answer. Serve it for lunch with a leafy salad, breadsticks, and cheese, or as a first course for dinner.

Ingredients

6 cups (1.4 L) vegetable broth

4 cloves fresh garlic, minced

1 cup (40 g) stale bread cubes

$1/4$ teaspoon salt

Several grinds black pepper

2 tablespoons (8 g) minced fresh Italian parsley

Bring the broth to a boil in a saucepan over medium-high heat, add the garlic, and simmer for 3 minutes. Add the bread cubes to the broth, along with the salt and pepper. Simmer 8 to 10 minutes, whisking occasionally as the bread breaks up and thickens the soup. Ladle into individual soup bowls and sprinkle each serving with parsley.

Yield: 4 servings

Each will have: 65 calories; 2 g fat; 1 g protein; 11 g carbohydrate; trace dietary fiber; 0 mg cholesterol.

Pastina and Pea Soup

Pastina is small dried pasta, commonly made in the shapes of stars, alphabet letters, or tiny circles. Serve this soup as a starter course or with a salad, bread, and cheese as a quick and delightful lunch or light supper.

Ingredients

4 cups (.95 L) vegetable broth

1 cup (130 g) frozen shelled peas

1 tablespoon (15 ml) extra-virgin olive oil

$^1/_2$ cup (80 g) diced yellow onion

3 cloves garlic, minced

$^1/_2$ cup (90 g) dried pastina

$^1/_2$ cup (120 ml) dry white wine

1 teaspoon dried tarragon

$^1/_4$ teaspoon salt

2 tablespoons (28 ml) half-and-half

$^1/_4$ cup (25 g) grated Parmesan cheese

Heat the vegetable broth in a microwave oven until steaming hot, about 2 minutes. Meanwhile, place the peas in a colander and run hot water over them for a few moments to melt off any ice crystals. Set aside.

Heat the olive oil in a large stockpot over medium heat. Add the onion and garlic and sauté for 1 minute, stirring frequently. Stir in the hot broth, cover, and increase the heat to high. Bring to a boil, then stir in the peas, pastina, wine, tarragon, and salt.

Cover and bring back to a boil, then simmer uncovered over medium heat for 4 to 5 minutes, until the pastina is al dente. Turn off the heat and stir in the half-and-half. Ladle into individual soup bowls and serve, passing the Parmesan cheese.

Yield: 4 servings

Each will have: 161 calories; 4 g fat; 6 g protein; 21 g carbohydrate; 2 g dietary fiber; 7 mg cholesterol.

Spinach and Couscous Soup with Kalamata Olives

Keep the ingredients for this soup on hand for an instant rainy-night meal. Serve with a salad of mixed greens tossed with feta cheese and Red Wine Vinaigrette (page 18).

Ingredients

4 cups (.95 L) vegetable broth

$1/3$ cup (60 g) dried couscous

1 teaspoon crushed garlic

$1/2$ teaspoon dried oregano

10 ounces (170 g) frozen chopped spinach

$1/4$ cup (35 g) kalamata olives, pitted and quartered

2 tablespoons (28 ml) half-and-half

$1/4$ cup (25 g) grated Parmesan cheese

1 lemon, cut into 4 wedges

Place the broth in a stockpot, cover, and bring to a boil over high heat. Add the couscous, garlic, and oregano, and continue to cook, uncovered, over high heat for about 5 minutes.

Meanwhile, place the spinach in a colander and rinse it well with hot water. Press it with the back of a wooden spoon, or squeeze with your hands, to remove as much excess moisture as possible.

Stir the spinach and kalamata olives into the soup and heat through for about 2 minutes. Turn off the heat and stir in the half-and-half. Ladle into individual soup bowls and sprinkle with Parmesan cheese. Serve immediately, passing the lemon wedges.

Yield: 4 servings
Each will have: 165 calories; 8 g fat; 6 g protein; 19 g carbohydrate; 3 g dietary fiber; 7 mg cholesterol.

Pasta in Broth with Pesto and Chard

This simple concoction is Italian comfort food, a great vegetarian substitute for your Aunt Stella's chicken soup. Capellini is very thin pasta, also sold as angel hair. The typical large bunch of chard will yield 6 cups (215 g) of diced leaves—and then some! Or you can use prewashed chopped chard in a bag from the supermarket. Pass Parmesan cheese, if you like, as a condiment.

Ingredients

7 cups (1.7 L) vegetable broth

2 cloves garlic, minced

$1/4$ teaspoon salt

4 ounces (115 g) dried capellini

6 cups (215 g) diced chard leaves

$1/4$ cup (65 g) basil pesto

$1/4$ teaspoon coarsely ground black pepper

Bring the broth, garlic, and salt to a boil over high heat in a covered stockpot. Break the capellini strands in half, then in half again, and add them to the boiling broth, along with the chard. Reduce the heat to medium-high and cook, uncovered, stirring frequently, for 5 minutes. Add the pesto and black pepper and stir to combine.

Yield: 4 servings

Each will have: 229 c alories; 9 g fat; 7 g protein; 30 g carbohydrate; 2 g dietary fiber; 4 mg cholesterol.

Egg-Lemon Soup with Spinach and Rice

This version of the Greek classic comes together in a flash because the rice is precooked. The sweeter Meyer lemons are essential here; they are readily available at well-stocked produce markets.

Ingredients

2 tablespoons (28 ml) extra-virgin olive oil

1 cup (160 g) diced yellow onion

4 cups (.95 L) vegetable broth

$1/4$ teaspoon crushed garlic

$1^1/2$ cups (295 g) cooked brown rice

2 large eggs

$1/3$ cup (80 ml) freshly squeezed Meyer lemon juice

$1/2$ teaspoon salt

Several grinds black pepper

8 ounces (225 g) prewashed baby spinach leaves

Heat the oil over medium heat in a stockpot and sauté the onion until it just begins to brown, about 5 minutes. Meanwhile, heat the vegetable broth in a microwave oven until steaming hot, about 2 minutes. Add the hot broth, garlic, and rice to the stockpot; cover; and bring to a simmer over high heat.

Meanwhile, place the eggs and lemon juice in a medium bowl and lightly beat with a fork. Slowly add about $1/2$ cup (120 ml) hot broth to the egg mixture and beat lightly to warm the eggs so they don't curdle when added to the soup. Repeat this process with two more $1/2$ cups of hot broth.

Turn off the heat and add the egg mixture to the soup, stirring gently to incorporate it. Add the salt, pepper, and spinach. Cover and allow the soup to stand in the pan for about 5 minutes before serving. Stir to combine and ladle into individual soup bowls.

Yield: 4 servings

Each will have: 232 calories; 11 g fat; 7 g protein; 28 g carbohydrate; 4 g dietary fiber; 106 mg cholesterol.

Cream of Zucchini and Fresh Basil Soup

This soup makes use of two of the garden's abundant summer crops—zucchini and basil. For the best texture, use zucchini that are on the small side, not the huge late-season ones. Serve the soup hot, or chill it for several hours and serve cold.

Ingredients

2 pounds (905 g) zucchini

1 tablespoon (14 g) unsalted butter

1 large white onion, diced

3 cups (710 ml) vegetable broth

$1/2$ cup (30 g) chopped fresh basil

1 teaspoon crushed garlic

$1/2$ teaspoon salt

$1/4$ teaspoon freshly grated nutmeg

Several grinds black pepper

$1/3$ cup (80 ml) half-and-half

Trim off and discard the root and stem ends of the zucchini. Dice the zucchini. Melt the butter in a stockpot over medium heat and sauté the onion for about 3 minutes, stirring frequently. Add the zucchini, broth, basil, garlic, salt, nutmeg, and pepper and bring to a boil over medium-high heat. Cover the pot and simmer until the zucchini is tender, about 5 minutes.

In a blender or food processor, puree the soup in small batches. Return the puree to the pot and add the half-and-half. Heat through briefly, but do not allow the soup to return to a boil.

Yield: 6 servings

Each will have: 95 calories; 4 g fat; 5 g protein; 9 g carbohydrate; 2 g dietary fiber; 11 mg cholesterol.

Tomato and Red Bell Pepper Puree with Wild Rice and Pine Nuts

Here is an antioxidant-rich feast that is flavorful and filling without overwhelming the palate. It makes a wonderful cool-weather lunch with the addition of crusty bread and a goat cheese or bean spread. Vacuum-packed cooked wild rice is available in some supermarkets and over the Internet.

Ingredients

1 can (28 ounces, or 785 g) diced tomatoes, undrained

1 jar (12 ounces, or 340 g) roasted red bell peppers, drained

1/4 cup (60 ml) dry white wine

1 tablespoon dried tarragon

1 clove garlic, coarsely chopped

1/2 teaspoon salt

1/4 teaspoon coarsely ground black pepper

1 cup (165 g) cooked wild rice

2 tablespoons (16 g) pine nuts

1/3 cup (80 g) lowfat sour cream

In a blender, puree the tomatoes with the roasted peppers, wine, tarragon, garlic, salt, and pepper. Transfer the mixture to a stockpot and add the wild rice. Bring to a strong simmer over medium-high heat, then reduce the heat to medium and simmer 5 minutes.

Meanwhile, place the pine nuts in a dry, heavy-bottomed skillet and toast over medium-high heat, stirring almost constantly, until they begin to brown. Immediately remove them from the pan and set aside to cool for a moment, then coarsely chop them.

Stir the sour cream into the soup, ladle into individual soup bowls, and garnish with the pine nuts.

Yield: 4 servings

Each will have: 165 calories; 4 g fat; 7 g protein; 27 g carbohydrate; 5 g dietary fiber; 4 mg cholesterol.

Chipotle Corn Chowder

This wonderfully rich and savory soup makes a fine main course on a chilly evening, with simple cheese quesadillas and a tangy salad served on the side. You may thaw the corn by simply transferring it from the freezer to the refrigerator overnight, or place it in a colander and rinse thoroughly with warm water just before using.

Ingredients

2 $1/2$ cups (570 ml) vegetable broth

1 pound (455 g) frozen corn kernels, thawed

1 cup (240 g) canned diced tomatoes, undrained

$1/2$ medium onion, diced

1 clove garlic, coarsely chopped

1 large canned *chipotle chile en adobo*

1 tablespoon (15 ml) adobo sauce (from can of chipotle chiles)

1 tablespoon dried oregano

$1/4$ teaspoon salt

$1/2$ cup (115 g) low-fat sour cream

$1/4$ cup (15 g) minced cilantro

1 lime, cut into 6 wedges

Place half the broth and half the corn kernels in a stockpot over medium-high heat. In a blender or food processor, combine the remaining stock and corn kernels with the tomatoes, onion, garlic, chipotle, adobo sauce, oregano, and salt. Process until fairly smooth. Transfer this mixture to the stockpot and bring to a simmer. Reduce the heat to medium and cook 5 minutes, stirring frequently to prevent scorching. Turn off the heat. Stir in the sour cream and cilantro until well blended. Offer a lime wedge with each serving.

Yield: 6 servings

Each will have: 127 calories; 3 g fat; 4 g protein; 23 g carbohydrate; 3 g dietary fiber; 4 mg cholesterol.

Garbanzo Bean and Spinach Stew

This stew is inspired by a Spanish dish called *garbanzos con espinacas*. Serve it with crusty bread and a dipping sauce of extra virgin olive oil and balsamic vinegar.

Ingredients

8 cups (1.9 L) vegetable broth

2 teaspoons crushed garlic

2 teaspoons paprika

$1/2$ teaspoon ground cumin

2 pinches saffron threads

Pinch of ground cloves

3 tablespoons (45 ml) extra-virgin olive oil

2 shallots, minced

2 fresh pear tomatoes, stemmed and diced

12 ounces (340 g) prewashed baby spinach leaves

2 cans (15 ounces, or 420 g, each) garbanzo beans

$1/2$ cup (75 g) golden raisins

Place the vegetable broth in a stockpot over high heat. Add the garlic, paprika, cumin, saffron, and cloves. Cover and bring to a boil.

Meanwhile, place a small skillet on the stovetop over medium-high heat and add the olive oil. Stir in the shallots and tomatoes and cook for 2 to 3 minutes. Set aside. When the broth has come to a boil, add the spinach and cook a minute or two, until the spinach wilts.

Place the beans in a colander, rinse, and drain. Stir the shallots and tomatoes into the soup, along with the garbanzo beans and raisins. Continue to cook over medium-high heat for about 3 minutes. Transfer to individual soup bowls and serve.

Yield: 6 servings
Each will have: 320 calories; 10 g fat; 10 g protein; 51 g carbohydrate; 9 g dietary fiber; 0 mg cholesterol.

VEGAN

Curried Okra and Black-Eyed Pea Stew

This hearty stew is an exotic way to enjoy two favorite foods of the American South, okra and black-eyed peas. Serve it with toasted *chapatis* (Indian flatbread) and a leafy salad for a perfect autumn meal.

Ingredients

1$^1/_2$ cups (360 g) canned diced tomatoes, undrained

1$^1/_2$ cups (355 ml) vegetable broth

$^1/_2$ cup (120 ml) light coconut milk

1 tablespoon Curry Powder (see recipe, page 29)

2 cloves garlic, minced

1 teaspoon ground cardamom

$^1/_2$ teaspoon salt

1 can (15 ounces, or 420 g) black-eyed peas

2$^1/_2$ cups (450 g) frozen sliced okra

1 carrot, finely diced

$^1/_3$ cup (60 g) dried couscous

In a large stockpot over medium-high heat, combine the tomatoes with the broth, coconut milk, curry powder, garlic, cardamom, and salt. Place the black-eyed peas in a colander, rinse, and drain. Add them to the soup, along with the okra and carrot. Bring to a simmer over medium-high heat, then add the couscous, reduce the heat to medium, and simmer for 5 minutes, stirring frequently. Ladle into individual soup bowls and serve.

Yield: 4 servings

Each will have: 247 calories; 3 g fat; 8 g protein; 47 g carbohydrate; 11 g dietary fiber; 0 mg cholesterol.

Tex-Mex Black Bean and Pumpkin Soup

Try this wonderful Southwest soup with corn tortillas or cornbread and a lime-seasoned salad

Ingredients

2 cans (15 ounces, or 420 g, each) black beans

1 tablespoon (15 ml) extra-virgin olive oil

1 medium yellow onion, diced

1 tablespoon pure chili powder

1 teaspoon ground cumin

1 teaspoon dried oregano

$1/2$ teaspoon salt

4 cups (.95 L) vegetable broth

2 teaspoons crushed garlic

1 can (15 ounces, or 420 g) pumpkin puree

$1/4$ cup (15 g) minced fresh cilantro

1 tablespoon (15 ml) freshly squeezed lime juice

Place the black beans in a colander, rinse briefly, and set aside to drain well.

Heat the olive oil over medium-high heat in a stockpot and sauté the onion, chili powder, cumin, oregano, and salt for 2 minutes, stirring frequently. Add the broth, black beans, and garlic and bring to a boil over high heat.

Stir in the pumpkin puree until well blended and simmer until heated through, about 3 minutes. Stir in the cilantro and lime juice and serve.

Yield: 6 servings

Each will have: 192 calories; 5 g fat; 9 g protein; 29 g carbohydrate; 11 g dietary fiber; 0 mg cholesterol.

Tuscan White Bean Soup with Garlic and Fresh Sage

This soup—known as *passato de fagiolo* in Italy—is pure comfort food. This vegetarian version is delightfully flavorful, thanks to the fresh sage, garlic, and Parmesan cheese. Round out the meal with a hearty salad, bread, and cheese.

Ingredients

3 cups (710 ml) vegetable broth
1 can (15 ounces, or 420 g) cannellini beans
4 cloves fresh garlic, minced
$1/4$ teaspoon salt
$1/4$ cup (60 ml) extra-virgin olive oil
$1/4$ cup (15 g) fresh sage
$1/3$ cup (35 g) grated Parmesan cheese
Several grinds black pepper

Place 2 cups (475 ml) vegetable broth in a stockpot, cover, and bring to a boil over high heat. Meanwhile, place the beans in a colander, rinse, and drain. Transfer them to a food processor, add the remaining 1 cup (235 ml) broth, and puree. Add the puree to the stockpot, along with 2 cloves of the garlic and the salt. Cover, reduce heat to medium-high and bring to a rapid simmer.

Meanwhile, place the olive oil in a small skillet over medium heat. Stir in the remaining 2 cloves garlic and the sage. Cook, stirring constantly, for about 1 minute. (Don't let the garlic brown or it will become bitter.) Pour this mixture into the stockpot, using a rubber spatula to remove all of the flavorful oil. Add the Parmesan cheese and black pepper and stir to incorporate. Heat through for a minute or two, then ladle into individual soup bowls and serve.

Yield: 4 servings

Each will have: 525 calories; 17 g fat; 28 g protein; 68 g carbohydrate; 16 g dietary fiber; 5 mg cholesterol.

Cannellini Bean and Tomato Soup with Chipotle Chiles

The *chipotle chiles en adobo* come in a can and are available at Mexican specialty markets and some supermarkets. Try this soup with Mushroom and Cheese Quesadillas (page 178) or warm corn tortillas.

Ingredients

1 can (15 ounces, or 420 g) cannellini beans

3 cups (710 ml) vegetable broth

2 tablespoons (28 ml) canola oil

1 small white onion, diced

1 cup (240 g) canned diced tomatoes, undrained

1 tablespoon (9 g) minced chipotle chiles en adobo

2 teaspoons crushed garlic

$1/2$ teaspoon salt

Place the beans in a colander, rinse, and drain. Place them in a stockpot, along with the vegetable broth. Cover the pan and bring to a boil over high heat, reduce heat to medium-high, and continue to simmer.

Meanwhile, heat the oil in a skillet over medium-high heat. Add the onion and sauté for 2 to 3 minutes. Stir in the tomatoes, chiles, garlic, and salt. Continue to cook for 3 to 4 minutes, stirring occasionally, until somewhat reduced.

Use a potato masher to break up the beans. Stir in the tomato mixture and heat through for a minute or two. Ladle into individual soup bowls and serve.

Yield: 4 servings

Each will have: 255 calories; 8 g fat; 12 g protein; 36 g carbohydrate; 11 g dietary fiber; trace cholesterol.

Coconut Curry Soup
with Tofu, Rice, and Vegetables

This Indonesian-style soup is hearty and very warming—exotic comfort food at its most satisfying. Pass a bottle of Asian chili sauce to crank up the fire, if you wish.

Ingredients

3 cups (710 ml) vegetable broth

1 cup (235 ml) light coconut milk

1 tablespoon Curry Powder (see recipe, page 29)

1 tablespoon (15 ml) soy sauce

1 tablespoon (8 g) grated fresh ginger

5 ounces (140 g) firm tofu, diced

1$^{1}/_{2}$ cups (295 g) cooked brown or basmati rice

1 cup (100 g) sliced button mushrooms

1 cup (120 g) shredded carrot

$^{1}/_{2}$ small red onion, thinly sliced

$^{1}/_{2}$ cup (65 g) frozen peas

1 cup (105 g) fresh mung bean sprouts, rinsed and patted dry

$^{1}/_{4}$ cup (15 g) minced fresh cilantro

1 lime, cut into 4 wedges

Combine the broth, coconut milk, curry powder, soy sauce, and ginger in a stockpot and bring to a boil over high heat. Add the tofu, rice, mushrooms, carrot, and onion and return to a simmer. Reduce the heat to medium-high and cook 5 minutes. Stir in the peas and cook 2 minutes longer.

Ladle into bowls and top each serving with a portion of bean sprouts and a sprinkling of cilantro. Place a lime wedge on top of the bean sprouts, to be squeezed into the soup by each diner.

Yield: 4 servings

Each will have: 211 calories; 6 g fat; 8 g protein; 33 g carbohydrate; 5 g dietary fiber; 0 mg cholesterol.

VEGAN

Chinese Hot-and-Sour Soup

Here is a classic healing soup from China. It is light and delicious on its own, and it becomes a substantial meal in a bowl when ladled over hot cooked rice. Rice vinegar is sometimes mixed with salt and sugar when used to season sushi rice. In this recipe, it's important to use the unseasoned variety.

Ingredients

6 fresh shiitake mushrooms

1 tablespoon (15 ml) dark sesame oil

1 small yellow onion, diced

2 cloves garlic, minced

7 cups (1.7 L) vegetable broth

1 cup (120 g) shredded carrot

1 cup (125 g) diced zucchini

1 tablespoon (8 g) grated fresh ginger

4 ounces (115 g) firm tofu, cut into matchsticks

2 tablespoons cornstarch

5 tablespoons (75 ml) unseasoned rice vinegar

2 tablespoons (28 ml) soy sauce

$1/4$ teaspoon cayenne pepper

Remove the stems from the shiitakes and thinly slice them. In a stockpot, heat the oil over medium-high heat. Add the mushrooms, onion, and garlic, and sauté for 3 minutes. Add the broth, carrot, zucchini, and ginger and bring to a boil over high heat. Reduce the heat to medium and stir in the tofu. Simmer for 5 minutes.

Meanwhile, whisk together the cornstarch, vinegar, soy sauce, and cayenne until the cornstarch is dissolved. Stir it into the simmering soup and cook until the broth is somewhat thickened, about 1 minute. Serve immediately.

Yield: 4 servings

Each will have: 157 calories; 7 g fat; 4 g protein; 23 g carbohydrate; 3 g dietary fiber; 0 mg cholesterol.

CHAPTER SEVEN

15-MINUTE
SANDWICHES
AND WRAPS

Almost every culture on the planet uses bread of some kind as a daily staple, so variations on the sandwich have evolved nearly everywhere. These dishes are casual, convenient, and easy to pack for lunch on the run. And cleanup is a snap!

Once you've practiced with our rolled and wrapped recipes, you can use the same techniques to create endless variations using your favorite ingredients. One of the beauties of the sandwich is that it is endlessly versatile and can be tailored to personal tastes.

The recipes here include both hot and cold sandwiches and use a variety of breads and wrappers. Some are suitable for light appetites; some are hearty and filling. The flavor combinations are inspired by many international cuisines.

Broiled Curry Portobello Mushroom Burgers with Chutney Sauce (page 112–113), Rice Wrap with Seasoned Tofu and Enoki Mushrooms (page 115), and Tempeh Sloppy Joes (page 110) suggest the range of our offerings. Which one would you like to have for lunch?

HERE ARE OUR SECRETS FOR GREAT-TASTING SANDWICHES

We have suggested specific condiments for some sandwiches, but feel free to substitute your favorite specialty mustards or other flavor enhancers.

~~~

Dark and chewy whole-grain breads are complex-carbohydrate foods, delivering vitamins and minerals, fiber, and essential amino acids. Pasty white breads, on the other hand, are refined carbs—the kind many health experts tell us to avoid.

~~~

Fresh bread makes all the difference in a tasty sandwich. If you don't eat bread often, keep part of the loaf in the freezer and the rest in the refrigerator. This prevents it from going stale or eventually growing mold as it sits on a warm counter.

Grilled sandwiches can be cooked on an outdoor gas grill, indoor stovetop grill, or countertop electric grill. The countertop models that close over the sandwich will cook both sides at once because they heat up on the top and the bottom—a great time-saver.

~~~

Frequently used seasonings and condiments—such as basil pesto, mayonnaise, and curry powder—are available in all major supermarkets, but they are simple and economical to make at home and keep on hand. See Chapter 2, "Seasonings, Condiments, and Simple Sauces" (page 16), for these useful recipes.

~~~

You can easily cook beans, grains, and vegetable stock from scratch. See "Preparing Frequently Used Ingredients" on page 234 to learn how.

Curry Tofu Egg Salad Sandwiches

You can keep this sandwich filling in the refrigerator for 2 to 3 days, so it makes a great make-ahead sandwich spread. It is also good served with crackers or vegetable slices. If you hard-boil a few eggs whenever you bring a dozen home from the market, they will be at the ready for quick recipes like this one.

Ingredients

8 ounces (225 g) firm tofu

2 large hard-boiled eggs

$1/2$ cup (115 g) low-fat mayonnaise

$1/4$ cup (15 g) minced fresh Italian parsley

1 teaspoon crushed garlic

1 teaspoon Curry Powder (see recipe
   page 29)

Pinch of salt

8 slices spelt, rye, or whole wheat bread

4 butter lettuce leaves

Slice the tofu and place the slices on paper towels to drain off any excess moisture. Peel the hard-boiled eggs and place them in a medium bowl with the tofu slices. Use a potato masher to mash the eggs and tofu.

Wrap It Up!

Our recipes provide specific blueprints for special sandwiches, but you don't need a recipe to make the quickest wraps of all. Keep a variety of tortillas, chapatis, and artisan breads on hand, tightly bagged in the refrigerator to extend their freshness. When hunger strikes, simply grab a wrapper, add a spoonful of beans, some fresh veggies and a drizzle of salad dressing, and you're good to go!

In a separate bowl, stir together the mayonnaise, parsley, garlic, curry powder, and salt. Add this to the tofu-and-egg mixture. Stir to combine.

Place half of the slices of bread on your work surface. Spread with equal amounts of the tofu mixture. Top with a lettuce leaf. Top with the other slice of bread, cut in half, and transfer to serving plates.

Yield: 4 servings

Each will have: 443 calories; 31 g fat; 16 g protein; 32 g carbohydrate; 6 g dietary fiber; 116 mg cholesterol.

Southwest Tofu Club Sandwiches

This hearty vegan club sandwich delivers lots of flavor and texture contrasts, and the presentation is very appetizing. Invite your best buddy over for lunch. Carrot sticks would be welcome on the side, along with a whole pickled jalapeño pepper if you like things hot and spicy.

Ingredients

6 slices whole-grain bread

1 teaspoon ground cumin

$1/2$ tablespoon freshly squeezed lime juice

$1/2$ teaspoon crushed garlic

$1/8$ teaspoon salt

Few grinds of black pepper

$1/2$ medium Haas avocado, diced (see page 240)

4 ounces (115 g) baked tofu, barbeque or savory flavor

4 paper-thin slices red onion

1 can (4 ounces, or 115 g) whole mild green chiles

2 red lettuce leaves

1 tablespoon Tofu Mayonnaise (see recipe, page 22)

Toast the bread until well browned. Meanwhile, place the cumin in a skillet over medium-high heat and stir constantly as it toasts for about 30 seconds. Transfer it to a bowl and add the lime juice, garlic, salt, and pepper. Add the avocado and mash with a fork to achieve a coarse (not smooth) consistency. Set aside. Cut the tofu into thin strips and set aside.

Lay 2 slices of toasted bread out on your work surface. Spread the avocado mixture evenly over the bread and top with sliced onions. Add a piece of toasted bread to each sandwich, then add the tofu strips in an even layer. Slit the whole green chiles open so they can lie flat. Add a whole green chile to each sandwich and top with a lettuce leaf. Spread the mayo on the remaining 2 slices of toasted bread and use them to top the sandwiches. Cut each sandwich in half and transfer to serving plates.

Yield: 2 servings

Each will have: 637 calories; 23 g fat; 23 g protein; 97 g carbohydrate; 18 g dietary fiber; 2 mg cholesterol.

Grilled Sourdough Sandwiches with Fresh Mozzarella, Tomato, and Pesto

Though this is a high-fat indulgence, on occasion it really hits the spot. Fresh mozzarella is packaged in water in a plastic container. Look for it in the deli section or cheese case of your supermarket. If you can find it, we prefer buffalo mozzarella. For this recipe, use the larger mozzarella balls, not the bocconcini size.

Ingredients

8 slices sourdough bread

$1/2$ pound (225 g) fresh mozzarella cheese, drained and thinly sliced

2 plum tomatoes, cored and thinly sliced

$1/2$ cup (130 g) Basil Pesto (see recipe, page 23)

2 tablespoons (28 ml) extra-virgin olive oil

Preheat the grill to medium. Arrange 4 slices of the bread on your work surface and top with equal amounts of mozzarella cheese. Add equal amounts of the tomato slices. Place the remaining 4 slices of bread on the work surface. Coat one side of the slices with pesto and use them to top the sandwiches.

Brush both sides of the sandwiches with oil and place them on the grill. Grill 4 to 8 minutes, depending on what type of grill you are using, turning if necessary to grill both sides. Remove from the grill, cut in half, and transfer to serving plates.

Yield: 4 servings

Each will have: 536 calories; 36 g fat; 22 g protein; 31 g carbohydrate; 2 g dietary fiber; 59 mg cholesterol.

Cheddar Cheese Melt with Roasted Peppers and Endive

Choose a whole-grain European-style rye bread and a sharp Cheddar cheese for this sandwich. The slight bitterness of endive is a great flavor note with the tangy cheese and sweet peppers.

Ingredients

8 slices dark rye bread

2 tablespoons (30 g) whole-grain mustard

4 cups (480 g) loosely packed grated Cheddar cheese

1 jar (7.25 ounces, or 203 g) roasted red bell peppers

16 endive leaves

Preheat your grill to medium. Arrange 4 slices of the bread on your work surface and spread equal amounts of mustard on one side of each slice. Using half the cheese, top the slices with equal amounts of cheese. Arrange equal amounts of the peppers on top of the cheese, then equal amounts of endive. Top with the remaining cheese, then with the remaining 4 slices of bread. Place on the grill, and grill 4 to 8 minutes, depending on what type of grill you are using, turning if necessary to grill both sides. Remove from the grill, cut in half, and transfer to serving plates.

Yield: 4 servings

Each will have: 646 calories; 40 g fat; 35 g protein; 37 g carbohydrate; 6 g dietary fiber; 119 mg cholesterol.

VEGAN

Grilled Tempeh Sandwiches

Serve this sandwich with your favorite mayonnaise, mustard, or ketchup. Tempeh is a dense soy product, so it's very filling, especially when served on a hearty whole-grain bread. Pass a tray of pickles and olives, if desired.

Ingredients

1 package (8 ounces, or 225 g) soy tempeh

1 tablespoon (15 ml) soy sauce

1 tablespoon (15 ml) dark sesame oil

2 teaspoons crushed garlic

8 slices spelt, rye, or whole wheat bread

1 medium tomato, sliced

4 butter lettuce leaves

Preheat the grill to medium. Carefully slice the tempeh crosswise to create 4 thin slices of equal size. In a shallow baking dish, mix together the soy sauce, sesame oil, and garlic. Place the tempeh slices in the soy sauce mixture and turn to coat. The tempeh will immediately soak up the marinade. Place on the grill, and grill for 3 to 4 minutes, then turn carefully and continue to grill for 3 to 4 more minutes.

Arrange the slices of bread (toasted, if you like), tomato slices, and lettuce leaves on a large platter. Remove the tempeh slices from the grill and place them on a warmed plate. Allow diners to create their own sandwiches, passing the condiments.

Yield: 4 servings

Each will have: 293 calories; 10 g fat; 17 g protein; 38 g carbohydrate; 4 g dietary fiber; 0 mg cholesterol.

Tempeh Sloppy Joes

This healthy and hearty rendition of the old favorite will still please kids and adults alike. The tempeh mimics the texture of ground meat and the flavors are mild and delicious. It's not a super-saucy version, so it can be picked up and eaten like a sandwich, rather than with a knife and fork.

Ingredients

1 tablespoon (15 ml) extra-virgin olive oil

1 package (8 ounces, or 225 g) soy tempeh, finely diced

1 cup (160 g) diced white onion

2 teaspoons dried oregano

2 teaspoons pure chili powder

$1/2$ teaspoon salt

2 cups (480 g) canned diced tomatoes, undrained

$3/4$ cup (175 ml) vegetable broth

1 can (4 ounces, or 115 g) diced green chiles

1 teaspoon crushed garlic

2 tablespoons (32 g) tomato paste

4 whole-grain burger buns

$3/4$ cup (90 g) shredded Cheddar cheese

2 cups (140 g) finely shredded green cabbage

Heat the oil in a sauté pan over medium-high heat. Add the tempeh, onion, oregano, chili powder, and salt and sauté, stirring frequently, for 3 minutes. Add the tomatoes, broth, green chiles, garlic, and tomato paste and bring to a simmer. Cover and cook for 5 minutes, while you toast the buns.

Place the bottom half of a toasted bun on each serving plate. Top with one-fourth of the tempeh mixture, then with one-fourth of the cheese and cabbage. Top with the other half of the bun. Make the rest of the sandwiches in the same fashion.

Yield: 4 servings

Each will have: 431 calories; 17 g fat; 24 g protein; 49 g carbohydrate; 8 g dietary fiber; 22 mg cholesterol.

Pita Sandwiches with Pinto Beans and Green Chiles

Serve this fusion-inspired pocket bread sandwich with the Smooth Cilantro Salsa on page 27 for a special treat, or use your favorite prepared smooth salsa.

Ingredients

1 can (15 ounces, or 420 g) pinto beans, drained

1 teaspoon crushed garlic

$1/4$ teaspoon pure chili powder

$1/8$ teaspoon ground cumin

$1/8$ teaspoon salt

1 can (4 ounces, or 115 g) diced green chiles

$1^1/2$ cups (225 g) grated mozzarella cheese

4 cups (140 g) shredded lettuce

4 whole-wheat pita bread rounds

Place the pinto beans, garlic, chili powder, cumin, and salt in a blender. Add 2 tablespoons (28 ml) of water and pulse to puree. Place in a bowl and stir in the diced green chiles.

Place the grated cheese and shredded lettuce in serving bowls. Cut the pocket breads into halves and wrap them in a clean dish towel. Place them in the microwave and heat for about 1 minute. Transfer them to a serving platter. Allow diners to fill their pita bread halves with beans, cheese, and lettuce. Top with your favorite salsa.

Yield: 4 servings

Each will have: 410 calories; 13 g fat; 21 g protein; 56 g carbohydrate; 10 g dietary fiber; 38 mg cholesterol.

Broiled Curry Portobello Mushroom Burgers with Chutney Sauce

The large round caps of portobello mushrooms are a perfect fit for burger buns. Serve these "burgers" with a vegetable salad like Green Bean Salad with Asian Flavors (see recipe, page 74). Feel free to substitute cilantro for the mint, if you have some on hand.

Ingredients

$^2/_3$ cup (160 g) plain nonfat yogurt

$^1/_3$ cup (85 g) prepared mango chutney, chopped if chunky

2 tablespoons (8 g) minced fresh mint

4 large portobello mushrooms

2 large red onions

$1^1/_2$ tablespoons (25 ml) extra-virgin olive oil

1 tablespoon (15 ml) balsamic vinegar

1 teaspoon Curry Powder (see recipe, page 29)

$^1/_4$ teaspoon salt

4 whole-grain burger buns

1 cup (70 g) finely shredded Napa cabbage

Preheat the broiler. In a bowl, stir together the yogurt, chutney, and mint until well combined. Set aside.

Cut off the stems of the mushrooms. Wipe or brush any visible dirt from the mushrooms, but don't rinse them under water. Peel the onions, discard the root ends, and cut each of them crosswise into 4 thick slices.

In a small bowl, combine the oil, vinegar, Curry Powder, and salt. Rub or brush the mushroom caps and the cut surfaces of the onions with this mixture.

Place the mushrooms and onions on a baking sheet and broil about 4 inches from the heat source until they are well browned on one side, about 3 minutes. Carefully turn the vegetables over and continue cooking until they are tender, about 3 to 5 minutes.

Meanwhile, toast the buns until well browned. Place the bottom half of a toasted bun on each serving plate and spread with about 2 tablespoons of the yogurt mixture. Top each one with a mushroom cap and 2 onion slices. Mound on one-fourth of the cabbage. Spread equal amounts of the remaining yogurt mixture on the other half of the buns and use them to top the sandwiches.

Yield: 4 servings
Each will have: 317 calories; 8 g fat; 12 g protein; 55 g carbohydrate; 8 g dietary fiber; 1 mg cholesterol.

Pita Sandwiches with Sprouted Beans, Cucumbers, and Tahini Mint Sauce

This sandwich is a nutrition powerhouse. The sprouted beans called for in this recipe are available in natural food stores, generally packaged in a plastic bag or clear plastic box. If you are accustomed to sprouting your own beans at home, all the better!

Ingredients

1 teaspoon paprika

1 teaspoon ground cumin

$^1/_3$ cup (80 g) plain nonfat yogurt

2 tablespoons (30 g) sesame tahini

2 tablespoons (28 ml) freshly squeezed lemon juice

$^1/_4$ teaspoon salt

$^1/_4$ teaspoon coarsely ground black pepper

$^1/_4$ cup (15 g) minced fresh mint leaves

6 ounces (170 g) sprouted mixed beans

1 cup (135 g) finely diced English cucumber

$^1/_4$ cup (40 g) minced red onion

4 whole-wheat pita bread rounds

2 cups (70 g) shredded lettuce

Put the paprika and cumin in a small, heavy skillet and toast over medium-high heat for just 30 seconds or so, stirring constantly. Transfer the spices to a large bowl and add the yogurt, tahini, lemon juice, salt, and pepper. Whisk until smooth, then stir in the mint. Add the sprouted beans, cucumber, and onion and stir to combine.

Cut the pita breads in half, and use your fingers to carefully separate the layers of bread to create 8 half-round pockets. Place a portion of the sprouted-bean filling in each pocket and top with some shredded lettuce.

Yield: 4 servings

Each will have: 273 calories; 6 g fat; 12 g protein; 47 g carbohydrate; 7 g dietary fiber; trace cholesterol.

Rice Wrap with Seasoned Tofu and Enoki Mushrooms

Once you get the hang of using Asian rice wrappers, you will want to come up with variations on this filling. Look for the wrappers in an Asian market; they are dry and packaged like tortillas. Pass tempura dipping sauce, also sold in Asian markets, if desired.

Ingredients

1 package (8 ounces, or 225 g) honey-sesame baked tofu

3 medium carrots

1 medium cucumber

6 rice wrappers

3 ounces (100 g) enoki mushrooms

3 tablespoons (45 ml) sweet chili sauce

Cut the tofu into thin matchsticks and briefly set aside. Grate the carrots and set aside. Peel the cucumber and cut in half lengthwise. Use a spoon to scoop out the seeds. Cut the cucumber into long matchstick pieces. Trim the bottom end from the mushrooms and separate them.

Place a large shallow bowl on the countertop and fill it with warm water. Slide a rice wrapper into the bowl for about 45 seconds. Remove to the countertop. Place one-sixth of the tofu, carrot, cucumber, and mushrooms in the center of the wrapper. Drizzle with one-sixth of the sweet chili sauce and roll up burrito-style. Repeat these steps with the remaining ingredients. Cut each wrap into thirds and place on a serving platter.

Yield: 6 servings

Each will have: 150 calories; 2 g fat; 7 g protein; 26 g carbohydrate; 2 g dietary fiber; 3 mg cholesterol.

VEGAN

Fresh Soybean, Avocado, and Seaweed Rice Wrap

This combination of traditional Asian flavors provides a very nutritious and satisfying lunch or light supper. If you want to carry one of these with you for a healthy lunch on the go, wrap it tightly in plastic wrap and refrigerate until serving time.

Ingredients

$^1/_4$ cup (15 g) dried hijiki seaweed

$^2/_3$ cup (170 g) fresh or frozen shelled green soybeans (edamame)

1 tablespoon (15 ml) freshly squeezed lemon juice

2 teaspoons soy sauce

1 teaspoon dark sesame oil

$^1/_8$ teaspoon cayenne

$^1/_2$ medium Haas avocado, diced (see page 240)

2 whole-wheat tortillas

1 cup (195 g) cooked brown rice

$^1/_2$ cup (35 g) finely shredded red or green cabbage

Place the hijiki in a glass or ceramic bowl, cover with 1 cup (235 ml) of water, and microwave on high for 1 minute. Set aside while you prepare the other ingredients.

If using frozen soybeans, place them in a saucepan with $^1/_3$ cup (80 ml) water, cover, and cook over medium-high heat for 3 minutes. Drain and set aside.

In a bowl, stir together the lemon juice, soy sauce, sesame oil, and cayenne. Add the avocado and stir gently to combine.

Lay the tortillas out flat on your work surface. Place half of the rice and soybeans on each wrapper, making a mound in the center. Lift the hijiki out of its soaking water, shake to remove excess water, and place a portion on each mound of rice. Add a portion of the avocado, scraping all the flavorful sauce out of the bowl. Add cabbage.

Fold up the bottom of each tortilla to overlap the filling, then turn in one side and roll up tightly, burrito-style.

Yield: 2 servings
Each will have: 579 calories; 22 g fat; 21 g protein; 78 g carbohydrate; 9 g dietary fiber; 0 mg cholesterol.

CHAPTER EIGHT

15-MINUTE
SAUTÉS AND
STIR-FRIES

The sizzle of ingredients as they hit a hot wok or skillet releases an instant cloud of fragrance that fills the house and heightens everyone's dinner anticipation.

Sautés made entirely of vegetables make excellent side dishes, while those incorporating beans, tofu, or tempeh can be a meal's main attraction. Eat these dishes all by themselves for a low-carb, high-nutrient feast, or combine them with a rice or pasta side dish for a heartier meal.

We suggest braising for some of the recipes in this chapter. This method calls for some liquid—generally stock, wine, or water—to be added after the initial sauté. The pan is then covered to finish the cooking. Another standard technique you will learn here is to thicken pan juices with arrowroot powder or cornstarch, as the Chinese do in their classic stir-fry dishes.

A few of our recipes don't call for any oil. In these cases, a small amount of vegetable stock or water is used instead. This method is called steam-sautéing, which is a fat-free way to prevent food from sticking to the pan as it cooks. It is especially appropriate for dishes that incorporate high-fat ingredients later in the cooking process, such as Curry-Sautéed Peppers with Chutney Cream (page 128).

We have looked mainly to the Far East for inspiration in this chapter, but dishes like Sherry-Sautéed Broccoli with Walnuts and Fresh Oregano (page 123) and Provencal Vegetable Stir-Fry with Fresh Basil (page 131) will take you on delicious excursions into other international cuisines.

POINTERS FROM THE PROS

FOLLOW THESE GUIDELINES FOR PERFECT SAUTÉS AND STIR-FRIES.

For best results when stir-frying, use a cooking oil with a high smoke point, such as canola, which has the added advantage of being high in healthy monounsaturated fat.

Trimmed and chopped vegetables in a bag, sometimes sold as stir-fry mixes, are available fresh or frozen and are great time-savers.

When sautéing or stir-frying foods at high temperatures, stir them frequently to prevent scorching.

All of these sautés and stir-fries can be served with the starch of your choice. Brown and basmati rice, soba noodles, bulgur, and couscous are some classic accompaniments for these dishes.

Precooked brown and jasmine rice have become widely available, either frozen or vacuum-packed. If your local grocer doesn't carry these convenient products, you can request that they be ordered. Better yet, cook a big batch of rice at home and keep it on hand in the refrigerator for a few days, reheating some in the microwave just before your stir-fry is ready to be served. It's easy to cook beans, grains, and vegetable stock from scratch. See "Preparing Frequently Used Ingredients" on page 234 to learn how.

Frequently used seasonings and condiments— such as basil pesto, mayonnaise, and curry powder—are available in all major supermarkets, but they are simple and economical to make at home and keep on hand. See Chapter 2, "Seasonings, Condiments, and Simple Sauces" (page 16), for these useful recipes.

Sautéed Spinach with Garlic

The preparation of this dish is simplicity itself. The only significant task is washing and chopping the spinach, but in the age of prewashed supermarket greens in a bag, you can even avoid that. Suit yourself about the amount of garlic—as you can see, we like to use a lot. You may substitute any of your favorite greens for the spinach.

Ingredients

$1/2$ tablespoon (8 ml) extra-virgin olive oil

3 cloves garlic, minced

$1 1/2$ pounds (680 g) prewashed baby
spinach leaves

$1/4$ teaspoon salt

1 teaspoon apple cider vinegar

In a large sauté pan, heat the oil over medium heat. Add the garlic; stir and sauté for 1 minute. Add the spinach to the pan, sprinkle on the salt, and toss the mixture with tongs until all the spinach wilts. Don't cook it too long or it will release all its liquid and the garlic will be left behind in the juice when you serve the spinach. Turn off the heat, add the vinegar, toss again, and serve.

Yield: 4 servings

Each will have: 45 calories; 2 g fat; 4 g protein; 5 g carbohydrate; 3 g dietary fiber; 0 mg cholesterol.

Why Wok?

Stir-frying is an ancient technique for cooking foods fast; the Chinese mastered it centuries ago. A wok is the traditional Chinese cooking vessel used for stir-frying. It is shaped like a big bowl to provide lots of surface area, so foods cook quickly as they are tossed about in the red-hot pan. Woks are generally inexpensive, and we recommend that you invest in one. If you don't have a wok, however, you can get similar results by using a large sauté pan or a cast-iron skillet. You can keep the food moving with the curved-edged spatula that came with your wok, stainless steel tongs, or two long-handled wooden spoons.

Sweet-and-Sour Braised Kale with Carrots

For this recipe, we use a mandoline to cut the carrot into paper-thin slices. An Asian specialty market that sells cooking implements is a good place to find an inexpensive version of this time-saving tool. If you don't have one, finely dice the carrot or substitute $1^1/_2$ cups (180 g) of the packaged shredded carrots, available in the produce section of the supermarket. If using fresh kale, rather than the pre-washed bagged variety, cut out and discard the thickest portions of the stems before chopping the leaves.

Ingredients

1 tablespoon (15 ml) apple cider vinegar

1 tablespoon (20 g) blackstrap molasses

1 tablespoon (15 ml) canola oil

1 cup (160 g) diced red onion

1 large carrot, very thinly sliced

$^1/_4$ teaspoon salt

$^1/_8$ teaspoon ground black pepper

8 cups (520 g) chopped kale, loosely packed

Stir together 1 cup (235 ml) of water, vinegar, and molasses and set aside.

Heat the oil in a large sauté pan over medium-high heat. Add the onion, carrot, salt, and pepper and sauté, stirring frequently, for 1 minute.

Mound the kale on top of the vegetables, pour in the vinegar-molasses mixture, and immediately cover the pan. Cook for 8 minutes, uncovering the pan once to stir the kale midway through the cooking time.

Remove the lid and continue to cook until there is very little liquid left in the pan, about 2 minutes.

Yield: 4 servings

Each will have: 133 calories; 4 g fat; 5 g protein; 22 g carbohydrate; 4 g dietary fiber; 0 mg cholesterol.

Sherry-Sautéed Broccoli with Walnuts and Fresh Oregano

During the winter months, fresh local broccoli from the farmers' market is full of flavor. For this recipe, purchase about 1 pound (455 g), or an equivalent amount of prewashed and bagged florets. This sauté tastes great served over brown rice. See pages 236–237 for rice-cooking instructions or reheat pre-cooked rice.

Ingredients

2 tablespoons (28 ml) dry sherry

1 tablespoon (15 ml) extra-virgin olive oil

$1/2$ teaspoon crushed garlic

4 cups (280 g) chopped broccoli or broccoli florets

$1/4$ cup (30 g) chopped walnuts

2 teaspoons minced fresh oregano

$1/8$ teaspoon salt

Several grinds black pepper

1 lemon, cut into 4 wedges

Heat the sherry, olive oil, and garlic in a wok or sauté pan over medium-high heat with $1/2$ cup (120 ml) water. Add the broccoli, cover, and cook until it is fork-tender, about 6 to 8 minutes. (Pay attention to the steam coming out of the pan and add a tablespoon or two of water if the pan dries out before the broccoli is done.) Transfer the broccoli to a serving dish and add the walnuts, oregano, salt, and pepper. Toss until well combined. Offer a lemon wedge with each serving.

Yield: 4 servings

Each will have: 87 calories; 8 g fat; 2 g protein; 1 g carbohydrate; trace dietary fiber; 0 mg cholesterol.

Spicy Snow Pea Sauté
with Fermented Black Bean Sauce

The delicate edible pods called snow peas can be found at most supermarkets. Your grocer may carry the chili oil and fermented black beans, but an Asian specialty food store is probably a better bet. Plain basmati rice makes the perfect accompaniment. (See pages 236–237 for rice-cooking instructions, or reheat precooked rice.)

Ingredients

$1/2$ pound (225 g) snow peas

3 tablespoons (45 ml) dry sherry

1 teaspoon soy sauce

1 teaspoon dark sesame oil

$1/4$ teaspoon chili oil

$1/2$ teaspoon crushed garlic

4 ounces (115 g) sliced button mushrooms

$1^1/2$ teaspoons cornstarch

$1/4$ cup (60 ml) vegetable broth

1 cup (105 g) fresh mung bean sprouts

2 teaspoons minced fermented black beans

Pull off and discard the stem ends and strings of the snow peas and halve them crosswise at a slant. Place the sherry, soy sauce, sesame oil, chili oil, and garlic in a wok or large skillet over medium-high heat and add the mushrooms. Cover and cook for 2 minutes, then stir in the snow peas and cook for 3 minutes.

Meanwhile, dissolve the cornstarch in the broth. Add the bean sprouts and fermented black beans to the cooked snow peas, pour in the cornstarch mixture, and stir and cook until the sauce thickens, about 2 minutes longer.

Yield: 4 servings

Each will have: 80 calories; 2 g fat; 3 g protein; 11 g carbohydrate; 3 g dietary fiber; 0 mg cholesterol.

VEGAN

Baby Bok Choy with Lemon Miso Sauce

This member of the cabbage family is widely available in supermarkets and at farmers' markets. It has a delicate flavor that pairs well with miso and lemon. Juice from thin-skinned Meyer lemons is a must here—it is much less bitter than that of the thicker-skinned Eureka variety, the one commonly sold in grocery stores. Serve this fragrant side dish with plain basmati rice and a tofu entrée. (See pages 236–237 for rice-cooking instructions, or reheat precooked rice.)

Ingredients

1 pound (455 g) baby bok choy
$^1/_4$ cup (60 ml) freshly squeezed lemon juice
2 tablespoons (35 g) light-colored miso
1 teaspoon crushed garlic
1 tablespoon cornstarch

Place about 2 inches (5 cm) of water in a saucepan that has a tight-fitting lid and place a steamer tray in the pan. Put the pan on to boil over high heat. Slice the bok choy in half lengthwise and place on the steamer rack. Cook until fork-tender, about 5 to 7 minutes.

Meanwhile, in a small pan, whisk together the lemon juice, miso, garlic, and $^1/_4$ cup (60 ml) water. Cook over low heat, stirring often, until it is steaming hot. Place 2 tablespoons (28 ml) water in a small jar that has a tight-fitting lid and add the cornstarch. Shake to dissolve. Whisk the cornstarch mixture into the lemon juice mixture and cook until thickened, about 1 minute. Drain the bok choy and fan it out on a warmed serving platter. Drizzle evenly with the sauce and serve.

Yield: 6 servings
Each will have: 30 calories; 1 g fat; 2 g protein; 5 g carbohydrate; 1 g dietary fiber; 0 mg cholesterol.

VEGAN

Cauliflower Sautéed with Peaches and Cardamom

This subtle interplay of flavors is stupendous but to be enjoyed only in the summertime, when peaches are at their peak of sweetness. Try this fragrant dish with Curried Couscous with Peas and Garbanzo Beans (page 151).

Ingredients

4 cups (600 g) chopped cauliflower

2 medium shallots, peeled and slivered

$^1/_4$ teaspoon salt

$^3/_4$ pound (340 g) firmly ripe peaches (about 2 medium)

$^1/_2$ teaspoon ground cardamom

Several grinds black pepper

2 tablespoons (8 g) minced fresh Italian parsley

Combine the cauliflower, shallots, and salt with $^1/_3$ cup (80 ml) water in a large skillet. Cover and cook over medium heat for about 7 minutes, until the cauliflower is barely fork-tender.

Meanwhile, peel the peaches and slice the flesh from the pits into bite-sized chunks. Add to the cauliflower, along with the cardamom and pepper. Sauté, stirring frequently, for 2 minutes. Transfer to a serving bowl and garnish with the parsley.

Yield: 4 servings

Each will have: 58 calories; trace fat; 3 g protein; 13 g carbohydrate; 4 g dietary fiber; 0 mg cholesterol.

VEGAN

Green Beans with Ginger Mushroom Sauté

Any variety of fresh mushroom will work for this fantastic side dish, but we especially like the intense flavor of shiitake or morel mushrooms. It's great served with soba noodles.

Ingredients

1 pound (455 g) fresh green beans

2 teaspoons dark sesame oil

1 tablespoon (15 ml) mirin or dry sherry

1 teaspoon grated fresh ginger

1/4 pound (115 g) sliced mushrooms

1/4 cup (60 g) lowfat sour cream

1/4 cup (55 g) raw, unsalted, shelled sunflower seeds

Place about 2 inches (5 cm) of water in a saucepan that has a tight-fitting lid and place a steamer tray in the pan. Put it on to boil over high heat. Trim off the stem ends of the beans, remove the strings if necessary, and cut them at a slant into 1-inch (2.5-cm) pieces. Place them in the steamer tray and cook until just fork-tender, about 6 to 8 minutes.

Meanwhile, combine the oil, mirin, and ginger in a skillet over medium-high heat. Add the mushrooms and sauté for 5 minutes, stirring frequently. Turn off the heat and stir in the sour cream.

Drain the beans and place them in a warmed serving bowl. Add the mushroom mixture and toss to combine. Sprinkle with the sunflower seeds and serve.

Yield: 6 servings

Each will have: 88 calories; 5 g fat; 4 g protein; 8 g carbohydrate; 3 g dietary fiber; 2 mg cholesterol.

Curry-Sautéed Peppers with Chutney Cream

Any combination of sweet peppers will work for this simple, flavorful side dish. We like to use at least two colors for a prettier effect. You can add cooked garbanzo beans to the sauté for a heartier dish. Basmati Rice with Saffron and Cumin Seeds (page 157) is the perfect accompaniment.

Ingredients

$1^1/_2$ pounds (680 g) sweet peppers (such as Anaheim, gypsy, or red and yellow bells)

2 cloves garlic, minced

2 teaspoons curry powder

1 medium red onion, diced

$^1/_8$ teaspoon plus a pinch of salt, divided

$^1/_3$ cup (80 g) plain nonfat yogurt

$^1/_3$ cup (80 g) lowfat sour cream

2 tablespoons (30 g) mango chutney, chopped if chunky

$^1/_4$ cup (15 g) minced fresh cilantro

3 tablespoons (45 ml) dry sherry

Remove and discard the stems, seeds, and most of the inner white membrane of the peppers. Chop the peppers into bite-sized chunks.

In a sauté pan, combine the garlic and curry cowder with $^1/_4$ cup (60 ml) of water and bring to a simmer over medium-high heat. Add the peppers, onion, and $^1/_8$ teaspoon of the salt. Stir to combine, cover, and cook 4 minutes. Remove the lid, and continue to stir and cook, uncovered, until the peppers are browning a bit and there is very little liquid remaining in the pan, about 3 minutes.

Meanwhile, stir together the yogurt, sour cream, chutney, cilantro, and remaining pinch of salt. Set aside. Place the sherry in a small bowl and set aside.

When the peppers are done, pour in the sherry and stir rapidly to deglaze the pan. When the sherry has evaporated, add the yogurt mixture and stir to combine. Heat through for only about 30 seconds and serve.

Yield: 4 servings

Each will have: 126 calories; 1 g fat; 4 g protein; 22 g carbohydrate; 4 g dietary fiber; 4 mg cholesterol.

Carrots Sautéed with Pineapple and Rum

This dish is a simple and delicious way to eat your fill of nutritious carrots. It can be served hot or at room temperature. Mint leaves make a pretty garnish if you have some growing in the garden.

Ingredients

1 tablespoon (14 g) unsalted butter

3/4 pound (340 g) baby carrots

2 shallots, peeled and thinly sliced

Pinch of salt

Several grinds black pepper

1 can (8 ounces, or 225 g) unsweetened pineapple chunks, drained
(juice reserved)

1/3 cup (80 ml) pineapple juice (from canned pineapple)

2 tablespoons (28 ml) dark rum

Melt the butter in a wok or sauté pan over medium-high heat. Add the carrots, shallots, salt, and pepper and sauté for 3 minutes, stirring often.

Meanwhile, drain the pineapple over a bowl, setting aside 1/3 cup (80 ml) of the juice and refrigerating the rest for another use. Add the juice and rum to the carrots and immediately cover the pan. Cook for 5 minutes, then stir in the pineapple chunks and cook until heated through, about 2 minutes.

Yield: 4 servings

Each will have: 123 calories; 3 g fat; 1 g protein; 20 g carbohydrate; 2 g dietary fiber; 8 mg cholesterol.

Corn, Spinach, and Tomato Sauté with Rosemary and Garlic

These three treasures of the summer garden are delicious combined with Mediterranean seasonings. Our recipe calls on the convenience of frozen corn kernels. If you prefer to use fresh corn, it will take a little time to cut the kernels from the cobs, but the flavor and texture will be spectacular. You will need about 4 medium ears of corn to yield 2 cups (310 g) of kernels.

Ingredients

2 cups (320 g) frozen corn kernels

$1/2$ teaspoon dried rosemary

$1/8$ teaspoon dried red chili flakes

1 teaspoon crushed garlic

$3/4$ pound (340 g) fresh pear tomatoes, diced

$1/4$ teaspoon salt

12 ounces (340 g) prewashed baby spinach leaves

2 tablespoons (28 ml) half-and-half

2 tablespoons (10 g) grated Parmesan cheese

Place the corn in a colander and rinse briefly to melt off any ice crystals. Use a mortar and pestle or the back of a wooden spoon to lightly crush the dried rosemary and chili flakes.

Heat 3 tablespoons (45 ml) water in a skillet over medium heat with the rosemary, chili flakes, and garlic. When it begins to simmer, add the corn. Sauté, stirring frequently, for 3 minutes while you dice the tomatoes. Add the tomatoes and salt to the corn, then pile on the spinach. Cover and cook for 3 minutes.

Remove the lid and stir gently until everything is well distributed. If there is still watery liquid in the bottom of the pan, continue to cook, uncovered, stirring constantly, until almost all of it has evaporated. Turn off the heat and stir in the half-and-half and Parmesan cheese.

Yield: 6 servings

Each will have: 83 calories; 2 g fat; 4 g protein; 16 g carbohydrate; 3 g dietary fiber; 3 mg cholesterol.

VEGAN

Provençal Vegetable Stir-Fry with Fresh Basil

This great side dish is wonderfully fragrant and quite satisfying. It's delicious with Fresh Linguine with Garlic and Poppy Seeds (page 143).

Ingredients

1 tablespoon (15 ml) extra-virgin olive oil

1 medium onion, diced

3 cloves garlic, minced

$1/4$ teaspoon dried red chili flakes

3 cups (300 g) bite-size cauliflower florets

2 medium zucchini, diced

$1/2$ cup (120 g) canned diced tomatoes, undrained

2 tablespoons (28 ml) dry white wine

2 teaspoons Herbes de Provence (see recipe, page 29)

$1/4$ teaspoon salt

Several grinds black pepper

1 cup (160 g) frozen corn kernels

$1/3$ cup (20 g) lightly packed fresh basil leaves, torn into pieces

Heat the oil in a wok or heavy skillet over medium heat. Add the onion, garlic, and chili flakes, and stir and sauté for 1 minute. Add the cauliflower, zucchini, tomatoes, wine, Herbes de Provence, salt, and pepper. Cover tightly and cook for 5 minutes. Remove the lid, add the corn, and stir and sauté for 3 minutes. Stir in the basil and serve.

Yield: 6 servings

Each will have: 85 calories; 3 g fat; 3 g protein; 14 g carbohydrate; 4 g dietary fiber; 0 mg cholesterol.

VEGAN

Carrot, Shiitake, and Fresh Soybean Sauté

Here is a scrumptious way to enjoy three great health-enhancing foods of the Far East: soybeans, shiitake mushrooms, and ginger. Serve this with plain rice or pilaf, or enjoy it all by itself as a satisfying feast of Asian flavors.

Ingredients

8 fresh shiitake mushrooms

1 tablespoon (15 ml) canola oil

2 large carrots, diced

1 medium onion, diced

$1/2$ cup (120 ml) vegetable broth

2 cloves garlic, minced

2 tablespoons (16 g) grated fresh ginger

1 teaspoon soy sauce

$1/4$ teaspoon salt

$1^1/2$ cups (385 g) fresh or frozen shelled green soybeans (edamame)

2 teaspoons arrowroot powder

Discard the stems of the mushrooms and thinly slice the caps. Set aside.

Heat the oil in a wok or heavy skillet over medium-high heat. Add the carrots and onion and sauté for 2 minutes, stirring often. Add the mushrooms, vegetable broth, garlic, ginger, soy sauce, and salt. Stir to combine and bring to a simmer, then stir in the soybeans. Return to a simmer and cook, uncovered, for 5 minutes, stirring often.

Meanwhile, dissolve the arrowroot in 2 tablespoons (28 ml) cold water. At the end of the vegetable cooking time, stir in the arrowroot mixture and cook about 30 seconds, stirring constantly, until the liquid thickens slightly.

Yield: 4 servings

Each will have: 231 calories; 10 g fat; 14 g protein; 25 g carbohydrate; 7 g dietary fiber; 0 mg cholesterol.

Zucchini with Garlic and Chili Flakes

This humble summer squash lends itself to many different preparations. Here it becomes a slightly spicy side dish for Italian entrées.

Ingredients

4 medium zucchini
1/8 teaspoon dried red chili flakes
1 tablespoon (15 ml) extra-virgin olive oil
2 cloves garlic, minced
1/8 teaspoon salt

Discard the stems and root ends of the zucchini. Cut them in half lengthwise, then cut each piece crosswise into 1/2-inch (1.25-cm) slices. Use a mortar and pestle or the back of a wooden spoon to lightly crush the chili flakes.

Heat the oil in a wok or sauté pan over medium-high heat and add the zucchini, garlic, chili flakes, and salt. Stir and sauté until the zucchini is browning nicely, about 3 minutes, then add 1/2 cup (120 ml) of water and immediately cover the pan. Cook for 3 minutes, then remove the lid and cook until almost all the liquid has evaporated.

Yield: 6 servings

Each will have: 40 calories; 2 g fat; 2 g protein; 4 g carbohydrate; 2 g dietary fiber; 0 mg cholesterol.

Braised Tofu with Shiitake Mushrooms and Carrots

This dish is reminiscent of *sukiyaki*, the broth-based Japanese favorite that is typically made with beef. Serve it with plain brown or basmati rice. (See pages 236–237 for rice cooking instructions, or reheat pre-cooked rice.)

Ingredients

1 cup (235 ml) vegetable broth
2 tablespoons (28 ml) soy sauce
1 tablespoon (15 ml) mirin or
    cooking sherry
2 teaspoons dark sesame oil
12 fresh shiitake mushrooms
12 ounces (340 g) firm silken tofu, cubed
1 cup (125 g) baby carrots,
    halved lengthwise
1/2 cup (30 g) chopped cilantro

Whisk together the broth, soy sauce, mirin, and dark sesame oil in a shallow, broad sauté pan. Arrange the whole mushrooms, tofu, and carrots in a single layer in the broth and bring to a simmer over medium-high heat. Reduce the heat to medium-low and simmer for 3 minutes. Turn the tofu over and continue to simmer until the carrots are fork-tender, about 4 to 5 minutes. Top with cilantro and cover for about a minute, until the cilantro wilts.

Yield: 4 servings

Each will have: 143 calories; 5 g fat; 8 g protein; 17 g carbohydrate; 2 g dietary fiber; 0 mg cholesterol.

VEGAN

Hot and Sweet Tofu with Papaya

This sauté is full of delicious flavor surprises. Cutting the bell peppers and papaya takes a bit of time, but the cooking is a snap. Try it with Basmati Rice with Saffron and Cumin Seeds (page 157).

Ingredients

$1/4$ cup (60 ml) vegetable broth or water

2 tablespoons (28 ml) mirin or cooking sherry

2 tablespoons (28 ml) unseasoned rice vinegar

$1^1/2$ tablespoons (25 ml) soy sauce

1 teaspoon dark sesame oil

1 pound (455 g) firm tofu, diced

1 small red bell pepper

1 small green bell pepper

2 green onions

1 medium ripe papaya

1 tablespoon (15 ml) canola oil

$1/8$ teaspoon dried red chili flakes

In a medium bowl, whisk together the vegetable broth, mirin, rice vinegar, soy sauce, and sesame oil. Add the diced tofu and set aside to marinate for 5 minutes, stirring occasionally, while you prep the veggies.

Remove and discard the stems, seeds, and white membranes of the peppers and dice them. Cut the green onions into $1/2$-inch (1.25-cm) lengths, discarding the root tips and some of the green portion. Cut the papaya in half, lengthwise, and use a spoon to scoop out and discard the seeds. Peel the papaya using a sharp paring knife and dice it into 1-inch pieces.

Heat the canola oil in a wok or heavy skillet over medium-high heat and add the bell peppers and chili flakes. Sauté for 2 minutes, then add the tofu and its marinade (be careful—it will spatter). Cook for 2 minutes, then add the papaya and green onions. Stir gently and cook for another 2 minutes.

Yield: 6 servings

Each will have: 128 calories; 7 g fat; 7 g protein; 11 g carbohydrate; 2 g dietary fiber; 0 mg cholesterol.

Tofu with Mushrooms and Miso

This simple sauté, quickly concocted from favorite ingredients, will appear on your table frequently. Serve it with brown or basmati rice. (See pages 236–237 for rice cooking instructions or reheat pre-cooked rice.)

Ingredients

1 pound (455 g) firm tofu

2 tablespoons (35 g) light-colored miso

2 tablespoons (28 ml) canola oil

8 ounces (225 g) sliced button mushrooms

1 small white onion, diced

1 medium green bell pepper, diced

1 tablespoon dried basil

1 teaspoon crushed garlic

Pinch of salt

2 tablespoons (8 g) minced fresh Italian parsley

2 tablespoons (28 ml) cider vinegar

1 lemon, cut into wedges

Cut the tofu into $1/2$-inch (1.25-cm) cubes and blot with paper towels to remove any excess moisture. Whisk the miso into $1/4$ cup (60 ml) warm water until smooth, and set aside.

Heat the oil in a wok or heavy skillet over medium-high heat and add the mushrooms, onion, bell pepper, basil, garlic, and salt. Sauté for 5 minutes, stirring frequently. Add the tofu and stir and sauté for 2 minutes.

Add the dissolved miso to the skillet, along with the parsley and vinegar, and cook 2 minutes, stirring occasionally. Offer a lemon wedge with each serving.

Yield: 4 servings

Each will have: 204 calories; 13 g fat; 12 g protein; 14 g carbohydrate; 3 g dietary fiber; 0 mg cholesterol.

Tempeh Stir-Fry with Ginger and Lemon

This dish has a delicious tart ginger flavor. Serve it with plain basmati rice to soak up all the yummy sauce. (See pages 236–237 for rice cooking instructions or reheat pre-cooked rice.) If you can't find whole or presliced crimini mushrooms, it's fine to use the standard white buttons.

Ingredients

2 tablespoons cornstarch

$1/4$ cup (60 ml) freshly squeezed lemon juice

2 tablespoons (40 g) honey

2 tablespoons (35 g) light-colored miso

1 tablespoon (15 ml) soy sauce

1 tablespoon (8 g) grated fresh ginger

1 tablespoon (15 ml) canola oil

1 medium yellow onion, diced

4 cups (400 g) sliced crimini mushrooms

$2 1/2$ cups (175 g) chopped fresh broccoli

8 ounces (225 g) soy tempeh, cubed

1 can (8 ounces, or 225 g) sliced water chestnuts, drained

In a medium bowl, whisk the cornstarch into 1 cup (235 ml) water. Add the lemon juice, honey, miso, soy sauce, and ginger, and whisk to combine. Set aside.

Heat the canola oil in a wok or heavy skillet over medium-high heat. Add the onion and stir and sauté for 1 minute, then add the mushrooms, broccoli, tempeh, and water chestnuts. Stir the cornstarch mixture to recombine and add it to the pan. Increase the heat to high and cook until the sauce thickens, about 3 minutes.

Yield: 4 servings

Each will have: 285 calories; 9 g fat; 16 g protein; 41 g carbohydrate; 5 g dietary fiber; 0 mg cholesterol.

VEGAN

Tempeh with Curry Peanut Sauce

This colorful combination of ingredients creates a rich, satisfying meal. Shop for a prepared peanut sauce in any Asian specialty market, or make your own using the recipe on page 24. Serve over soba noodles or basmati rice. (See pages 236–237 for rice-cooking instructions, or reheat precooked rice.)

Ingredients

1 large carrot, diced

2 ribs celery, diced

2 tablespoons (28 ml) peanut oil

1 tablespoon Curry Powder (see recipe page 29)

1 tablespoon dried oregano

1 teaspoon pure chili powder

8 ounces (225 g) soy tempeh, diced

1 tablespoon (10 g) crushed garlic

2 tablespoons (30 ml) Asian Peanut Sauce (see recipe page 24)

1 lemon, cut into wedges

Dice the carrot and celery and set aside. Place the oil in a wok or heavy skillet and heat over medium heat. Add the Curry Powder, oregano, and chili powder. Stir to combine. Quickly add the tempeh, garlic, carrot, and celery, then stir in $^3/_4$ cup (175 ml) water and the peanut sauce. Cover and cook over high for about 6 to 8 minutes, until the vegetables are tender-crisp and the sauce has reduced somewhat, stirring frequently. Serve immediately, passing the lemon wedges.

Yield: 4 servings

Each will have: 226 calories; 14 g fat; 13 g protein; 16 g carbohydrate; 2 g dietary fiber; 0 mg cholesterol.

CHAPTER NINE

15-MINUTE
PASTA DISHES

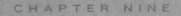

Pasta in one form or another is a staple in many countries throughout the world. Its versatility and hearty goodness make it a universal favorite. When you think there's nothing in the house to cook, pasta comes to the rescue. It can be combined with olive oil and any odds and ends of vegetables, beans, cheeses, and fresh or dried herbs for a quick and satisfying supper.

Some of our recipes call for fresh pasta. It cooks more quickly than dried and has a delicate texture that pairs especially well with light cream sauces. That said, dried pasta offers a wider variety of shapes and sizes, and if you use a couple of simple shortcuts—see "Pointers from the Pros" on page 140—you can cook any standard pasta within the 15-minute time frame.

We draw our pasta inspiration from many sources, including Italian and Asian traditions. But many of our recipes can best be called "fusion" cuisine, based on innovative combinations of ingredients and seasonings from a variety of cultures. It's the world on a plate!

PERFECT PASTA'S A SNAP WITH THESE SIMPLE TIPS.

For a fast start on pasta dishes, place several quarts of hot water in a stockpot, cover, and put it on to boil over high heat. Obviously, starting with hot water reduces the time it takes to boil.

For best results, stir the pasta a few times as it cooks, to keep the strands from sticking together or to the bottom of the pot.

Once the water has come to a boil, add the pasta and leave the lid off. This prevents the pot from boiling over.

When a recipe calls for draining the pasta, do so by carefully pouring it into a footed colander placed in the sink. Shake the colander to remove excess water before completing the dish as directed. Don't rinse the pasta unless you're planning to use it for a pasta salad and want to cool it quickly.

If you have an allergy to wheat, or just for a change of pace, try out the alternative pasta varieties—such as those made with spelt, corn, rice, or Jerusalem artichoke flour—that are available at natural food stores and some supermarkets.

Frequently used seasonings and condiments—such as basil pesto, mayonnaise, and curry powder—are available in all major supermarkets, but they are simple and economical to make at home and keep on hand. See Chapter 2, "Seasonings, Condiments, and Simple Sauces" (page 16), for these useful recipes.

You can easily cook beans, grains, and vegetable stock from scratch. See "Preparing Frequently Used Ingredients" on page 234 to learn how.

Orzo with Green Onions, Lemon, and Capers

Orzo are small ovals of pasta that have a delicate texture. They combine well with finely minced ingredients, like those in this recipe, to create a pretty as well as delicious side dish for Mediterranean entrées.

Ingredients

$1^1/_2$ cups (280 g) dried orzo
$1/_2$ teaspoon salt
6 green onions
1 tablespoon (15 ml) extra-virgin olive oil
2 cloves garlic, minced
$1/_4$ cup (60 g) lowfat sour cream
2 tablespoons (28 ml) freshly squeezed lemon juice
2 tablespoons (18 g) capers, drained and minced
1 tablespoon lemon zest
Several grinds black pepper

Fill a stockpot with about 8 cups (1.9 L) hot water, cover, and bring to a boil over high heat. Stir in the orzo and $1/_4$ teaspoon of the salt. Cover and bring to a rolling boil. Remove the lid, reduce the heat to medium, and cook, stirring occasionally, until al dente, about 6 minutes.

Meanwhile, mince the green onions, discarding the root tips and some of the green portion. Heat the oil in a sauté pan

---

"To the Tooth"

Italian cooks use the term *al dente* to describe pasta that has been perfectly cooked. The literal translation of this phrase is "to the tooth," meaning that the pasta offers just a hint of resistance when you bite into it. Undercooked pasta has a tough center and an unpleasant, starchy taste. But if it's cooked too long, pasta will break apart easily and turn to mush in the mouth. Test as you go and let your senses guide you. Soon it will become second nature to recognize perfectly cooked pasta.

---

over medium heat and sauté the garlic, green onions, and remaining $1/_4$ teaspoon of salt. Sauté, stirring almost constantly, for 2 minutes.

When the orzo is al dente, add $1/_2$ cup (120 ml) of the orzo cooking water to the green onions, then drain the orzo well. Add the orzo to the pan, along with the sour cream, lemon juice, capers, lemon zest, and black pepper. Stir over medium heat until everything is well combined, about 1 minute.

Yield: 6 servings
Each will have: 196 calories; 3 g fat; 6 g protein; 35 g carbohydrate; 2 g dietary fiber; 2 mg cholesterol

Simple Vermicelli Sicilian Style

The people of Sicily are so passionate about their native foods that even the local bus driver will share his favorite recipes! This Sicilian pasta takes little time to prepare. It can accompany a wide variety of dishes or suffice as a light main course with a hearty salad and bread on the side.

Ingredients

8 ounces (225 g) dried vermicelli
$1/8$ teaspoon dried red chili flakes
2 tablespoons (28 ml) extra-virgin olive oil
3 cloves garlic, minced
$1/4$ teaspoon salt

Put several quarts of hot water in a stockpot, cover, and bring to a boil over high heat. Add the vermicelli and cook, stirring occasionally, until al dente, about 7 to 8 minutes. Drain well and transfer to a warmed serving bowl.

Meanwhile, use a mortar and pestle or the back of a wooden spoon to lightly crush the chili flakes. Place the olive oil in a small sauté pan or skillet over medium heat. Add the garlic, chili flakes, and salt. Sauté until the garlic is barely browned, about 2 minutes. Pour the seasoned oil over the hot pasta in the bowl, using a rubber spatula to get all of it out of the pan. Toss until the pasta is well coated with the oil.

Yield: 4 servings
Each will have: 264 calories; 7 g fat; 5 g protein; 45 g carbohydrate; trace dietary fiber; 0 mg cholesterol.

Fresh Linguine with Garlic and Poppy Seeds

Here is a simple and delicious side dish pasta that pairs well with Broiled Eggplant with Dried Tomato Marinara (page 191). Poppy seeds quickly become stale if stored at room temperature; keep them in a tightly closed container in the freezer and they will stay fresh and flavorful for a long while.

Ingredients

12 ounces (340 g) fresh linguine

$1/2$ teaspoon salt

2 tablespoons (28 ml) extra-virgin olive oil

2 cloves garlic, minced

$1^1/2$ tablespoons (15 g) poppy seeds

$1/2$ cup (50 g) grated Parmesan cheese

Put several quarts of hot water in a stockpot, cover, and bring to a boil over high heat. Cut the linguine strands in half and stir them into the boiling water, along with $1/4$ teaspoon salt. Cook the linguine until barely al dente, about 3 to 4 minutes, stirring occasionally.

Meanwhile, heat the oil in a small sauté pan or skillet over medium heat and add the garlic. Cook, stirring constantly, until the garlic is barely browned, about 2 minutes. Stir in the poppy seeds and set aside if the linguine is not yet done.

When the linguine is done, ladle about 1 cup (235 ml) of its cooking water into the sauté pan. Add the remaining $1/4$ teaspoon salt and turn the heat back on to medium. Drain the pasta well and add it to the pan. Toss until the garlic and poppy seeds are evenly distributed and the noodles are coated with a light sauce. Turn off the heat, add the cheese, and toss to combine.

Yield: 4 servings

Each will have: 441 calories; 13 g fat; 16 g protein; 65 g carbohydrate; 2 g dietary fiber; 8 mg cholesterol.

Fresh Linguine with Light Tomato Cream Sauce

This dish is a delectable melding of savory ingredients. Garnish the finished dish with fresh basil leaves and lemon slices for a pretty presentation.

Ingredients

10 ounces (280 g) fresh linguine

1 tablespoon (15 ml) extra-virgin olive oil

1 teaspoon crushed garlic

1 can (28 ounces, or 785 g) diced tomatoes, undrained

$^1/_2$ cup (115 g) lowfat sour cream

$^1/_4$ cup (65 g) basil pesto

2 tablespoons (18 g) capers, drained and minced

2 tablespoons (16 g) pine nuts

$^1/_2$ cup (50 g) finely grated Parmesan cheese

Put several quarts of hot water in a stockpot, cover, and bring to a boil over high heat. Add the linguine and cook until al dente, about 3 to 4 minutes, stirring occasionally. Drain and transfer to a large, warmed serving bowl.

Meanwhile, heat the oil in a large sauté pan over medium-high heat and add the garlic. Stir for a moment, then add the tomatoes, bring to a rapid simmer, and cook until reduced to a medium sauce consistency, about 10 minutes. Turn off the heat and stir in the sour cream, pesto, and capers.

Pour the sauce over the hot pasta and toss to combine. Top with the pine nuts and serve, passing the Parmesan cheese.

Yield: 4 servings

Each will have: 496 calories; 15 g fat; 20 g protein; 70 g carbohydrate; 6 g dietary fiber; 22 mg cholesterol.

Creamy Linguine with Garlic, Peas, and Nutmeg

Quick, delicious, and satisfying, this dish is a real winner. Use freshly grated nutmeg for best results. Pass extra nutmeg and Parmesan cheese as condiments, if desired.

Ingredients

12 ounces (340 g) fresh linguine

$1^1/2$ cups (195 g) frozen peas

1 tablespoon (15 ml) extra-virgin olive oil

3 cloves garlic, minced

2 cups (475 ml) lowfat milk

$1/2$ teaspoon salt

$1/2$ teaspoon ground nutmeg

1 cup (100 g) finely grated Parmesan cheese

Put several quarts of hot water in a stockpot, cover, and bring to a boil over high heat. Add the linguine and cook for 3 minutes, stirring occasionally. Add the frozen peas and let stand with the heat off for 1 minute. Reserve a cup of the cooking water, then drain the pasta and peas and set them aside in a warm place if the sauce is not yet ready.

Meanwhile, heat the olive oil in a large sauté pan over medium-high heat. Add the garlic and sauté for 1 minute, then add the milk, salt, and nutmeg, and bring to a simmer. Reduce the heat to medium-low and simmer gently for 5 minutes.

Add the drained linguine and peas to the sauce and toss until the peas are well distributed and the pasta is well coated with sauce. Turn off the heat, add the Parmesan, and toss to combine.

Yield: 4 servings

Each will have: 463 calories; 13 g fat; 25 g protein; 61 g carbohydrate; 3 g dietary fiber; 83 mg cholesterol.

Fresh Linguine and Asparagus with Tarragon Cream Sauce

This fresh linguine will melt in your mouth! It's a wonderful pasta to prepare in the early spring, when asparagus first comes into season. Pass grated Parmesan cheese as a condiment, if desired. Use freshly grated nutmeg for this dish, if possible, for an intense flavor note.

Ingredients

1 pound (455 g) fresh asparagus

8 ounces (225 g) fresh linguine

2 tablespoons (28 g) unsalted butter

2 tablespoons (15 g) unbleached white flour

$1/4$ cup (60 ml) dry white wine

2 teaspoons dried tarragon

1 cup (235 ml) lowfat milk

$1/4$ teaspoon ground nutmeg

1 lemon, cut into wedges

Put several quarts of hot water in a stockpot, cover, and bring to a boil over high heat. Rinse the asparagus and snap off the tough ends. Cut the stalks at a slant into 1-inch (2.5-cm) pieces.

Add the linguine and asparagus to the boiling water. Cook, stirring occasionally, for 3 to 4 minutes, until the linguine is al dente and the asparagus is tender-crisp. Drain and transfer to a large, warmed serving bowl.

Meanwhile, melt the butter in a large skillet over medium heat. Add the flour and whisk until a thick paste forms. Add the wine and tarragon, then gradually add the milk, whisking to incorporate into a smooth sauce. Stir in the nutmeg.

Pour the sauce over the linguine and asparagus, tossing to combine well.

Yield: 4 servings

Each will have: 293 calories; 8 g fat; 12 g protein; 43 g carbohydrate; 3 g dietary fiber; 59 mg cholesterol.

Capellini with Tomatoes, Arugula, and Kalamata Olives

This combination of flavors is very savory and satisfying. It makes a wonderful springtime supper. Cream of Zucchini and Fresh Basil Soup (page 92) would be a great first course.

Ingredients

12 ounces (340 g) dried cappellini

1¹/₂ tablespoons (25 ml) extra-virgin olive oil

3 cloves garlic, minced

¹/₂ teaspoon dried red chili flakes

1 can (28 ounces, or 785 g) diced tomatoes, undrained

¹/₄ teaspoon salt

¹/₃ cup (35 g) finely chopped kalamata olives

4 cups (80 g) prewashed baby arugula leaves

Put several quarts of hot water in a stockpot, cover, and bring to a boil over high heat. Add the capellini and cook, stirring occasionally, until al dente, about 5 to 7 minutes. Drain well and set aside if the sauce is not yet done.

Meanwhile, heat the olive oil over medium heat in a large, heavy-bottomed skillet or sauté pan. Add the garlic and chili flakes and sauté for a minute, stirring constantly. Add the tomatoes and salt, increase the heat to medium-high, and simmer about 7 minutes, stirring frequently, until the sauce is somewhat reduced. Stir in the olives, then the arugula.

Add the pasta to the sauce in the sauté pan, toss to combine, and cook 1 minute.

Yield: 4 servings

Each will have: 434 calories; 8 g fat; 15 g protein; 76 g carbohydrate; 6 g dietary fiber; 0 mg cholesterol.

Capellini with Tomatoes and Fresh Shiitakes

Fresh shiitake mushrooms have a rich and distinctive flavor that is enhanced here by a very quick pan roasting. Pass grated Parmesan as a condiment, if you wish.

Ingredients

8 ounces (225 g) dried capellini

4 ounces (115 g) fresh shiitake mushrooms

2 tablespoons (28 ml) extra-virgin olive oil

1 cup (160 g) diced yellow onion

3 cloves garlic, minced

$1/2$ teaspoon salt

2 cups (480 g) canned diced tomatoes, undrained

$1/4$ cup (60 ml) dry red wine

1 tablespoon dried oregano

Several grinds black pepper

Put several quarts of hot water in a stockpot, cover, and bring to a boil over high heat. Add the capellini and cook, stirring frequently, until al dente, about 5 to 7 minutes. Drain well and set aside if the sauce is not yet done.

Meanwhile, remove and discard the stems of the shiitake mushrooms and dice the caps. Heat the oil in a large sauté pan over medium-high heat. Add the mushrooms and cook without stirring for 1 minute, then turn them and cook 1 minute longer. Add the onion, garlic, and $1/4$ teaspoon of the salt; stir and sauté for 1 minute. Add the tomatoes, wine, oregano, remaining $1/4$ teaspoon salt, and pepper. Bring to a simmer and cook for 5 minutes.

Add the pasta to the sauce in the sauté pan, toss to combine, and cook 1 minute.

Yield: 4 servings

Each will have: 416 calories; 8 g fat; 13 g protein; 75 g carbohydrate; 8 g dietary fiber; 0 mg cholesterol.

Fusilli with Roasted Red Bell Pepper Pesto

The pesto used here as a pasta sauce also could be spread on bread as an appetizer, stirred into broth with a few veggies to make a quick and delicious soup, or used to season hot cooked grains. Keep some on hand in the refrigerator for instant inspiration when dinner preparation time is short.

Ingredients

12 ounces (340 g) dried fusilli (corkscrew pasta)

1 jar (12 ounces, or 340 g) roasted red bell peppers, drained

2 tablespoons (28 ml) extra-virgin olive oil

1 tablespoon (15 ml) freshly squeezed lemon juice

$1/2$ teaspoon salt

Several grinds black pepper

$1/3$ cup (40 g) chopped walnuts

$1/3$ cup (20 g) fresh mint leaves, coarsely chopped

2 cloves garlic, coarsely chopped

$1/2$ cup (50 g) grated Parmesan cheese

Put several quarts of hot water in a stockpot, cover, and bring to a boil over high heat. Add the fusilli and cook, stirring occasionally, until al dente, about 8 to 9 minutes.

Meanwhile, place the red bell peppers in a blender with the olive oil, lemon juice, salt, and pepper. Puree. Add the walnuts, mint, and garlic and process until the mixture is homogeneous, scraping down the sides of the blender as needed. Transfer the pesto to a large serving bowl and set aside.

When the pasta is al dente, reserve 1 cup (235 ml) of the cooking water before draining it. Add $1/2$ cup (120 ml) of the cooking water to the pesto in the serving bowl and stir to combine. Drain the fusilli and add it to the bowl, top with the cheese, and toss until the pasta is evenly coated with the pesto. Add more cooking liquid, if necessary, to achieve a creamy consistency.

Yield: 6 servings

Each will have: 344 calories; 12 g fat; 13 g protein; 46 g carbohydrate; 3 g dietary fiber; 7 mg cholesterol.

Mushroom Stroganoff

This rich and creamy creation is a delicious indulgence. If possible, use sliced crimini mushrooms for this dish instead of the standard white button variety, for the extra flavor they provide.

Ingredients

6 ounces (170 g) egg noodles

4 tablespoons (55 g) unsalted butter

1 pound (455 g) sliced mushrooms

1/2 cup (80 g) chopped yellow onion

2 tablespoons (28 ml) dry white wine

1 teaspoon crushed garlic

1/4 teaspoon salt

2 tablespoons (15 g) unbleached flour

1 cup (235 ml) vegetable broth, heated in the microwave

1/2 cup (115 g) lowfat sour cream

2 tablespoons (30 g) catsup

Place several quarts of hot water in a stockpot, cover, and bring to a boil over high heat. Add the egg noodles and cook until al dente, about 5 minutes. Drain and transfer to a large, warmed serving bowl. If the sauce is not yet done, set the noodles aside.

Meanwhile, melt 2 tablespoons (28 g) butter in a sauté pan over medium-high heat and add the mushrooms, onion, wine, garlic, and salt. Sauté until the mushrooms are limp, about 5 minutes, stirring occasionally.

In a separate large saucepan over medium heat, melt the remaining 2 tablespoons (28 g) butter. Add the flour, then gradually add the hot stock, whisking to incorporate it into a smooth sauce. Whisk in the sour cream and catsup and cook until thickened, about 2 minutes, whisking constantly. Fold in the mushroom mixture.

Pour the hot sauce over the noodles and toss to combine well.

Yield: 4 servings

Each will have: 369 calories; 16 g fat; 11 g protein; 47 g carbohydrate; 3 g dietary fiber; 77 mg cholesterol.

Curried Couscous with Peas and Garbanzo Beans

Serve this fragrant dish with lemon wedges and additional yogurt on the side, if desired.

Ingredients

1¹/₂ cups (355 ml) vegetable broth

1 cup (175 g) dried couscous

2 green onions

1 tablespoon (15 ml) extra-virgin olive oil

¹/₂ tablespoon curry powder (see recipe page 29)

1 medium red bell pepper, diced

1 cup (130 g) frozen shelled peas

1 cup (240 g) cooked garbanzo beans

¹/₄ teaspoon salt

¹/₂ cup (125 g) plain nonfat yogurt

Place the broth in a saucepan over high heat and bring to a boil. Stir in the couscous, then immediately cover the pan and remove it from the heat. Set aside for 5 minutes without disturbing the lid.

Meanwhile, mince the green onions, discarding the root tips and some of the green portion. Heat the olive oil in a small skillet over medium-high heat, add the curry powder, and stir it around in the oil for about 30 seconds. Add the bell pepper and green onion; stir and sauté for 2 minutes. Add the peas, garbanzo beans, salt, and ¹/₃ cup (80 ml) of water; stir and sauté for 5 minutes. Remove from the heat and stir in the yogurt.

Transfer the couscous to a warm bowl, add the garbanzo bean mixture, and toss gently until all the ingredients are well distributed.

Yield: 8 servings
Each will have: 162 calories; 3 g fat; 7 g protein; 28 g carbohydrate; 3 g dietary fiber; trace cholesterol.

Couscous with Feta, Olives, and Walnuts

The tiny beads of pasta called couscous, native to Morocco, cook in 5 minutes flat. This dish combines many flavors of the Mediterranean. It is scrumptious with a fresh salad and/or a platter of sliced fresh tomatoes.

Ingredients

2 tablespoons (28 ml) extra-virgin olive oil

1 teaspoon crushed garlic

$^1/_4$ teaspoon salt

Several grinds black pepper

2 cups (350 g) dried couscous

3 green onions

$^1/_2$ cup (75 g) crumbled feta cheese

$^1/_4$ cup (25 g) finely chopped kalamata olives

$^1/_4$ cup (15 g) finely chopped fresh basil leaves

2 teaspoons lemon zest

3 tablespoons (45 ml) freshly squeezed lemon juice

$^1/_3$ cup (40 g) chopped walnuts

Bring 3 cups (710 ml) water to a boil in a medium saucepan. When the water boils, add 1 tablespoon of the olive oil, the garlic, salt, and pepper, then stir in the couscous. Immediately cover the pan and remove it from the heat. Set aside for 5 minutes without disturbing the lid.

Meanwhile, mince the green onions, discarding the root tips and some of the green portion. Place them in a serving bowl with the feta cheese, olives, basil, and lemon zest. Stir in the lemon juice and the remaining tablespoon of olive oil.

Fluff the couscous with a fork and add it to the feta mixture. Add the nuts and toss gently until all the ingredients are well distributed.

Yield: 6 servings

Each will have: 345 calories; 12 g fat; 11 g protein; 48 g carbohydrate; 4 g dietary fiber; 11 mg cholesterol.

Soba Noodles with Green Soybeans and Spicy Tahini Sauce

This dish is delicious and filling—a good choice at the end of a labor-intensive day. Serve your favorite steamed or sautéed green vegetable on the side. Frozen green soybeans (edamame) and buckwheat soba noodles are available at well-stocked supermarkets or Asian specialty food stores.

Ingredients

8 ounces (225 g) dried buckwheat soba
  noodles
2 cups (510 g) frozen shelled green soybeans (edamame)
1 cup (120 g) shredded carrots
1 cup (235 ml) vegetable broth
3 tablespoons (45 g) sesame tahini
1 tablespoon (15 ml) soy sauce
1 tablespoon (15 ml) unseasoned
  rice vinegar
1 tablespoon (8 g) grated fresh ginger
2 teaspoons granulated sugar
Pinch of cayenne pepper
4 green onions
1 teaspoon sesame seeds

Put several quarts of hot water in a stock-pot, cover, and bring to a boil over high heat. Add the soba noodles and stir gently. Bring back to a boil and cook for 5 minutes. Stir in the soybeans and carrots. Return to a boil and cook for 2 minutes.

Reserve 1 cup (235 ml) cooking liquid before draining the soba and vegetables. If the sauce is not yet done, transfer soba and vegetables to a warmed serving bowl and set aside.

Meanwhile, in a medium saucepan over medium-high heat, whisk together the broth, tahini, soy sauce, vinegar, ginger, sugar, and cayenne. Bring to a simmer, reduce the heat to low, and cook for 2 minutes. Stir half of the reserved cooking water into the sauce. Thinly slice the green onions, discarding the root tips and some of the green portion; set aside.

Add the tahini sauce to the serving bowl and toss gently until the soybeans are well distributed and the noodles are evenly coated with sauce. Add the remaining cooking water a little at a time, if necessary, to achieve a smooth and creamy consistency. Garnish with the green onions and sesame seeds.

Yield: 4 servings
Each will have: 485 calories; 16 g fat; 28 g protein; 67 g carbohydrate; 9 g dietary fiber; 0 mg cholesterol.

CHAPTER TEN

15-MINUTE
GRAIN DISHES

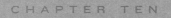

Grains are the hearty and wholesome heart of the vegetarian diet. They provide complex carbohydrates for sustained energy production, plus lots of essential vitamins, minerals, fiber, and amino acids.

Some grains—such as brown rice, barley, and buckwheat—take a long time to cook. Our recipes showcase the quicker-cooking varieties such as cornmeal, bulgur wheat, and quinoa, an ancient Peruvian grain that has been rediscovered and is now widely available.

Precooked rices—brown, jasmine, and wild—have expanded our repertoire of 15-minute grain dishes. These great convenience foods are available, either frozen or vacuum-packed, at many supermarkets. If yours doesn't carry them, ask that they be ordered. You also can find instant brown rice in most supermarkets next to the instant white rice boxes.

Although grains appear as ingredients in many recipes throughout this book, in this chapter they play a starring role. Recipes that combine grains with beans or soy products—such as Wild Rice with Mushrooms and Fresh Soybeans (page 162)—can serve as hearty, high-protein main dishes. Others are perfect as side dishes or for lighter appetites.

We hope the recipes in this chapter inspire you to make healthy whole grains a part of your daily meals.

HERE ARE SOME SUGGESTIONS TO HELP YOU ENJOY THE GOODNESS OF GRAINS.

When time permits, cook up a pot of rice, following the instructions on pages 236–237. It will keep for a few days in the refrigerator, ready to play a role in salads or soups, or serve as an instant side dish.

⌇

When you're using precooked rice, heat it in a microwave oven before adding it to a recipe.

⌇

We buy our grains in bulk at a natural food market and store them in airtight jars in a cool, dry cupboard. They will stay fresh this way for many months.

⌇

Whole grains can attract kitchen moths. If you see any evidence of webbing or flying insects in a jar of grain, immediately dispose of the grain in your outside trash and sterilize the jar in your dishwasher or by scrubbing with soap and hot water.

Frequently used seasonings and condiments— such as basil pesto, mayonnaise, and curry powder—are available in all major supermarkets, but they are simple and economical to make at home and keep on hand. See Chapter 2, "Seasonings, Condiments, and Simple Sauces" (page 16), for these useful recipes.

⌇

You can easily cook beans, grains, and vegetable stock from scratch. See "Preparing Frequently Used Ingredients" on page 234 to learn how.

VEGAN

Basmati Rice with Saffron and Cumin Seeds

Including its final steaming time after you turn off the heat, it takes 20 minutes from start to finish to cook basmati rice. But since this fragrant rice is the perfect accompaniment for any curry entrée, we decided to bend the rules just a bit and include it in this book. (And remember, you can always use precooked basmati rice and stay well within your fifteen minutes!)

Ingredients

1 cup (185 g) uncooked white basmati rice
Pinch of saffron threads
$^1/_4$ teaspoon cumin seeds
$^1/_2$ teaspoon salt

Place the rice in a fine-mesh strainer and rinse with cold water for about 1 minute to remove some of its surface starch. Place a dry saucepan over medium heat and add the saffron threads and cumin seeds. Stir and toast for about 30 seconds, then add the rice and stir until the saffron color is evenly distributed. Add $1^3/_4$ cups (410 ml) of hot water and the salt and bring to a simmer. Cover and cook 10 minutes. Turn off the heat and allow the rice to stand in the covered pot for 5 minutes. Transfer the rice to a serving bowl, using a fork to fluff up the grain.

Yield: 4 servings

Each will have: 154 calories; 1 g fat; 4 g protein; 32 g carbohydrate; 0 g dietary fiber; 0 mg cholesterol.

Confused about Carbs?

The low-carb diet trend is said to be ending, but it's leaving a lot of confusion in its wake. Although the science of carbohydrate metabolism is complex, the bottom line is easy to grasp. The carb-culprits we should avoid are processed (white) flour and/or sugar. These "simple" carbohydrates lurk in doughnuts, cakes, cookies, and candy bars; sodas and soft drinks; processed cereals and breakfast bars; and white-flour crackers and breads. Minimizing such foods in your diet is an important strategy for achieving and maintaining good health and optimal body weight.

The "complex" carbohydrates in whole grains and vegetables, on the other hand, are essential to a healthy diet. They offer important vitamins, minerals, fiber, and amino acids and should make up a substantial portion of our daily calories. They are filling without packing a massive calorie punch. The grain recipes in this chapter (and elsewhere in this book) will help you experience the benefits of a high-but-healthy-carb diet.

Basmati Rice with Pesto and Peas

This rice dish may be served as a main course, along with a substantial salad, or as a side dish with your favorite tofu entrée.

Ingredients

2 cups (260 g) frozen shelled peas

2 tablespoons (28 g) unsalted butter

$1/2$ cup (80 g) diced red onion

$1/2$ cup (115 g) lowfat sour cream

$1/4$ cup (65 g) basil pesto

2 cups (320 g) cooked basmati rice, reheated in the microwave

Place the peas in a colander and rinse them under hot water to thaw and warm them. Set aside to drain.

Melt the butter in a small skillet over medium-high heat and add the onion. Stir and sauté for 3 minutes, then stir in the sour cream and pesto and reduce the heat to low. Cook until heated through, about 2 minutes, stirring constantly. Place the hot rice in a bowl, add the peas and the pesto mixture, and toss to combine.

Yield: 4 servings

Each will have: 335 calories; 15 g fat; 10 g protein; 39 g carbohydrate; 6 g dietary fiber; 26 mg cholesterol.

VEGAN

Fried Rice with Tofu and Veggies

Here is a simple and delicious one-dish lunch or dinner. Don't let the number of ingredients deter you—it really comes together very quickly once you have the veggies prepped. Be sure to start with cold rice, which is less likely to stick to the pan than hot. Frozen brown rice that has been thawed in the refrigerator for a few hours is a perfect choice.

Ingredients

1 cup (235 ml) vegetable broth

1 tablespoon (15 ml) soy sauce

1 tablespoon (15 ml) canola oil

2 teaspoons dark sesame oil

1 teaspoon ground ginger

1 teaspoon crushed garlic

Pinch of cayenne pepper

$^1/_2$ cup (80 g) diced yellow onion

$^1/_2$ cup (60 g) shredded carrots

8 ounces (225 g) sliced button mushrooms

$^1/_2$ pound (225 g) firm tofu, diced

2 cups (140 g) diced green cabbage

1 cup (130 g) frozen shelled peas

4 cups (640 g) cooked brown or basmati rice, cold

In a small bowl, stir together the broth, soy sauce, canola oil, sesame oil, ginger, garlic, and cayenne.

Heat a wok or sauté pan over medium-high heat for a minute or so, then pour in $^1/_4$ cup (60 ml) of the broth mixture and add the onion, carrots, and mushrooms. Stir-fry for 2 minutes. Add the tofu, cabbage, peas, and another $^1/_4$ cup (60 ml) of the broth mixture. Stir-fry for 3 minutes.

Add the rice and onions and the remainder of the broth mixture. Stir and toss the rice with the other ingredients until everything is well combined and steaming hot, about 3 minutes.

Yield: 6 servings

Each will have: 240 calories; 7 g fat; 8 g protein; 38 g carbohydrate; 4 g dietary fiber; 0 mg cholesterol.

Pumpkin and Brown Rice "Risotto" with Fresh Rosemary

This quick dish has the characteristic creamy texture of a classic slow-stirred risotto, but it is far from traditional. It pairs well with Sautéed Spinach with Garlic (page 121) or simple steamed broccoli.

Ingredients

1 tablespoon (15 ml) extra-virgin olive oil

$^1/_4$ cup (15 g) minced fresh parsley

2 tablespoons minced fresh rosemary leaves

2 cloves garlic, minced

$1^1/_2$ cups (355 ml) vegetable broth

2 cups (450 g) canned pumpkin puree

4 cups (640 g) cooked brown rice

$^1/_2$ teaspoon salt

$^1/_2$ cup (50 g) grated Parmesan cheese

1 tablespoon (15 ml) freshly squeezed lemon juice

Heat the oil in a large saucepan over medium heat. Add half the parsley (reserve the rest for garnish), the rosemary, and the garlic. Stir and sauté for 30 seconds, then add the broth and pumpkin and stir to combine. Add the rice and salt and cook over medium heat, stirring frequently to prevent scorching, until very hot, about 8 minutes. Stir in the cheese and lemon juice, transfer to a serving dish, and garnish with the reserved parsley.

Yield: 6 servings

Each will have: 232 calories; 6 g fat; 7 g protein; 39 g carbohydrate; 5 g dietary fiber; 5mg cholesterol.

Spicy Black-Eyed Peas and Rice with Onions

This is our vegetarian variation of a classic dish of the American South, Hoppin' John. Season it with plenty of hot pepper sauce, as they do in Louisiana. It's a great main dish and the perfect match for Sweet-and-Sour Braised Kale with Carrots (page 122).

Ingredients

2 tablespoons (28 ml) extra-virgin olive oil

2 medium yellow onions, diced

2 cloves garlic, minced

$1/2$ teaspoon salt

$1/4$ teaspoon coarse black pepper

1 can (15 ounces, or 420 g) black-eyed peas

1 cup (160 g) cooked brown or white rice

$1/2$ cup (120 ml) vegetable broth

Louisiana hot pepper sauce (such as Tabasco), to taste

Heat the oil in a large sauté pan over medium-high heat and add the onions, garlic, $1/4$ teaspoon salt, and the pepper. Sauté, stirring frequently, until the onions and garlic are browning nicely, about 5 minutes.

Meanwhile, place the black-eyed peas in a colander, rinse, and drain. When the onions are done, add the black-eyed peas, rice, broth, and remaining $1/4$ teaspoon salt. Cover and cook for 3 minutes. Stir in hot pepper sauce, according to taste, and serve.

Yield: 4 servings

Each will have: 236 calories; 8 g fat; 5 g protein; 37 g carbohydrate; 7 g dietary fiber; 0 mg cholesterol.

Wild Rice with Mushrooms and Fresh Soybeans

The chewy texture, dark color, and nutty flavor of wild rice complement fresh green soybeans (edamame) very well. You can buy cooked wild rice in vacuum-sealed bags and fresh or frozen shelled edamame at well-stocked supermarkets or natural food stores.

Ingredients

$1/2$ tablespoon extra-virgin olive oil

8 ounces (225 g) sliced button mushrooms

$1/2$ medium onion, diced

1 clove garlic, minced

1 tablespoon dried basil

$1/4$ teaspoon salt

$1/4$ teaspoon coarsely ground black pepper

2 cups (330 g) cooked wild rice

$1^1/2$ cups (385 g) fresh or frozen shelled green soybeans (edamame)

$1/2$ cup (120 ml) vegetable broth or water

$1/4$ cup (30 g) finely chopped oil-packed dried tomatoes

Heat the oil in a large sauté pan over medium-high heat and add the mushrooms, onion, garlic, basil, salt, and pepper. Sauté for 3 minutes, stirring frequently, then add the wild rice, soybeans, and broth. Stir to combine, cover, and cook for 5 minutes, then stir in the dried tomatoes and serve.

Yield: 4 servings
Each will have: 280 calories; 10 g fat; 18 g protein; 35 g carbohydrate; 7 g dietary fiber; 0 mg cholesterol.

Microwaved Polenta with Whole Corn, Green Chiles, and Cheese

If you're not familiar with polenta, the savory cornmeal mush of Italy, this recipe is a delicious introduction. Traditionally, it requires a long spell of stirring at the stove. This quick version takes its flavor inspiration from the American Southwest and has quite a bit of zip. Reduce the amount of green chiles if you want a milder dish.

Ingredients

3/4 cup (105 g) uncooked polenta

1 teaspoon pure chili powder

1/2 teaspoon salt

1 cup (160 g) frozen corn kernels

1 can (4 ounces, or 115 g) diced green chiles

1 teaspoon crushed garlic

1 cup (115 g) shredded Cheddar cheese

In a large glass or ceramic bowl, stir together 1 3/4 cups (410 ml) of hot water, the polenta, chili powder, and salt. Microwave, uncovered, for 6 minutes.

Meanwhile, place the corn in a strainer and rinse with hot water for about 30 seconds to thoroughly defrost it. When the polenta has cooked for 6 minutes, whisk 1 cup (235 ml) water into it, then stir in the corn, green chiles, and garlic. Microwave, uncovered, for an additional 6 minutes. Add the cheese and stir briskly with a wooden spoon as it melts into the polenta.

Yield: 4 servings

Each will have: 257 calories; 10 g fat; 11 g protein; 31 g carbohydrate; 3 g dietary fiber; 30 mg cholesterol.

Grilled Polenta with Blue Cheese

The colors in this dish are festive and appetizing, and the aroma is scrumptious. For a wonderful patio dinner, serve it with simple steamed vegetables and Fennel and Radicchio Salad with Balsamic Vinaigrette (page 75). Use your favorite store-bought marinara sauce, or make some according to our recipe on page 25.

Ingredients

1 pound (455 g) prepared polenta log

1 tablespoon (15 ml) extra-virgin olive oil

$1/4$ cup (65 g) Tomato Marinara Sauce (see recipe, page 25)

$1/2$ cup (60 g) crumbled blue cheese

Preheat the grill to high. Slice the polenta log into 8 slices of equal thickness. Brush both sides of the slices with olive oil, or use olive-oil spray to coat them lightly. Place the slices on the grill and cook for 2 to 3 minutes. Turn and top with equal amounts of the marinara sauce and blue cheese. Cook until the cheese is bubbly, 2 to 3 minutes.

Yield: 4 servings

Each will have: 178 calories; 9 g fat; 6 g protein; 19 g carbohydrate; 1 g dietary fiber; 13 mg cholesterol.

Broiled Polenta with Tomato Sauce and Mozzarella Cheese

This is lovely served the first course or as part of an Italian-themed meal. Use your favorite store-bought marinara sauce, or make some according to our recipe on page 25.

Ingredients

1 pound (455 g) prepared polenta log

1 cup (250 g) Tomato Marinara Sauce (see recipe, page 25)

1¹/₂ cups (170 g) shredded mozzarella cheese

Preheat the broiler. Slice the polenta log into 12 slices of equal thickness. Place half of the marinara sauce in a shallow baking dish and layer the polenta slices on top. Sprinkle half of the cheese over the polenta, then top with the remaining marinara sauce. Sprinkle with the remaining cheese and place under the broiler, about 6 inches (15 cm) from the heat source. Broil until the polenta is hot and the cheese is melted and lightly browned, about 5 minutes.

Yield: 6 servings

Each will have: 167 calories; 8 g fat; 8 g protein; 15 g carbohydrate; 1 g dietary fiber; 25 mg cholesterol.

VEGAN

Curried Veggie Sauté with Quinoa

Quinoa is a high-protein grain originally cultivated by the Aztecs in ancient times. Seek it out in a natural food market or from an Internet grocer. The tiny grains have a distinctive flavor and texture that will bring variety to your daily ration of whole grains.

Ingredients

$^1/_2$ cup (85 g) uncooked quinoa

$^1/_8$ teaspoon plus $^1/_4$ teaspoon salt

1 tablespoon (15 ml) canola oil

1 cup (160 g) finely diced red onion

1 medium red bell pepper, finely diced

2 cups (140 g) finely diced green cabbage

1 tablespoon Curry Powder (see recipe, page 29)

1 cup (130 g) frozen shelled peas

$^1/_2$ cup (120 ml) vegetable broth or water

Place the quinoa in a fine-mesh strainer and rinse thoroughly. Combine in a saucepan with 1 cup (235 ml) of water and $^1/_8$ teaspoon of the salt. Cover and bring to a boil over high heat, then reduce the heat to medium-low and cook 10 minutes.

Meanwhile, heat the oil in a sauté pan over medium-high heat and add the onion, bell pepper, cabbage, curry powder, and remaining $^1/_4$ teaspoon salt. Stir and sauté for 3 minutes, then add the peas and broth, cover the pan tightly, and cook for 5 minutes.

Add the cooked quinoa to the vegetables, including any quinoa cooking liquid that remains in the saucepan. Stir to combine well, then cover the pan and allow to stand for about 1 minute before serving, to infuse the quinoa with flavor.

Yield: 4 servings

Each will have: 177 calories; 5 g fat; 6 g protein; 28 g carbohydrate; 6 g dietary fiber; 0 mg cholesterol.

Provencal Braised Asparagus with Quinoa and Olives

Here is a savory and satisfying combination, perfect for lunch on a pretty spring day.

Ingredients

$^3/_4$ cup (130 g) uncooked quinoa

$^1/_4$ teaspoon plus $^1/_8$ teaspoon salt

$1^1/_4$ pounds (560 g) fresh asparagus

1 tablespoon (15 ml) extra-virgin olive oil

2 cloves garlic, minced

1 teaspoon Herbes de Provence (see recipe, page 29)

Several grinds black pepper

$^1/_4$ cup (45 g) finely chopped roasted red bell pepper

$^1/_4$ cup (25 g) finely chopped kalamata olives

1 tablespoon (15 ml) freshly squeezed lemon juice

Place the quinoa in a fine-mesh strainer and rinse thoroughly. Combine in a saucepan with $1^1/_2$ cups (355 ml) of water and $^1/_4$ teaspoon salt. Cover and bring to a boil over high heat, then reduce the heat to medium-low and cook 10 minutes.

Meanwhile, trim off and discard about 2 inches (5 cm) of the tough ends of the asparagus and cut the spears at a slant into 1-inch (2.5-cm) pieces.

Heat the oil in a sauté pan over medium-high heat and add the asparagus, garlic, herbes de Provence, remaining $^1/_8$ teaspoon salt, and pepper. Sauté for 2 minutes, stirring frequently, then pour in $^1/_3$ cup (80 ml) water and immediately cover the pan. Cook over medium-high heat for 3 minutes. Turn off the heat under the asparagus and remove the lid from the pan.

Add the cooked quinoa to the asparagus, including any quinoa cooking liquid that remains in the saucepan. Add the roasted red bell pepper, olives, and lemon juice. Stir to combine, then cover the pan and allow to stand for about 1 minute before serving, to infuse the quinoa with flavor.

Yield: 4 servings
Each will have: 199 calories; 7 g fat; 8 g protein; 30 g carbohydrate; 6 g dietary fiber; 0 mg cholesterol.

Bulgur with Spinach and Feta Cheese

There's something especially satisfying about the combination of grains, greens, and garlic. Leftovers taste great; Just heat them briefly in the microwave.

Ingredients

2 cups (475 ml) vegetable broth

1 tablespoon dried basil

2 teaspoons crushed garlic

$1/4$ teaspoon salt

Several grinds black pepper

5 ounces (140 g) frozen chopped spinach (2 cups)

1 cup (140 g) uncooked bulgur wheat

$1/2$ cup (75 g) crumbled feta cheese

Place the broth in a saucepan and add the basil, garlic, salt, and pepper. Cover and bring to a boil over medium-high heat.

Meanwhile, place the spinach in a strainer and rinse it with warm water until it is thoroughly thawed, about 1 minute. Press gently with a wooden spoon or squeeze with your hands to remove excess liquid.

When the broth boils, stir in the bulgur and spinach. Cover, reduce the heat to medium-low, and cook 10 minutes, stirring once midway through the cooking time. Transfer to a serving bowl and stir in the feta cheese.

Yield: 4 servings

Each will have: 201 calories; 5 g fat; 8 g protein; 32 g carbohydrate; 8 g dietary fiber; 16 mg cholesterol.

Bulgur in Tomato Sauce with Thyme and Allspice

This unusual bulgur preparation has a Middle Eastern flair. The consistency is dense and the flavor deeply savory.

Ingredients

4 green onions

1 tablespoon (15 ml) extra-virgin olive oil

1/2 teaspoon crushed garlic

1/2 teaspoon dried thyme

1/2 teaspoon ground allspice

1/2 teaspoon ground black pepper

1 cup (140 g) uncooked bulgur

1 can (15 ounces, or 420 g) diced tomatoes, undrained

1/4 teaspoon salt

Mince the green onions, discarding the root tips and some of the green portion. Heat the oil over medium heat in a saucepan. Add the green onions, garlic, thyme, allspice, and pepper. Sauté for 1 minute, then add the bulgur, tomatoes, salt, and 1 cup (235 ml) of hot water. Cover and bring to a simmer over medium-high heat, reduce the heat to medium-low, and cook for 10 minutes, stirring once midway through the cooking time. Transfer to a serving bowl and stir well to combine the ingredients.

Yield: 4 servings

Each will have: 206 calories; 4 g fat; 6 g protein; 36 g carbohydrate; 9 g dietary fiber; 0 mg cholesterol.

CHAPTER ELEVEN

15-MINUTE TORTILLA DISHES

Tortillas are the humble and wholesome heart of Mexican cuisine. Simple as they are, they lend themselves to a variety of delicious uses. This chapter features flour, corn, and sprouted-grain varieties, folded, rolled, and layered with savory fillings for quick and easy meals.

Although the roots of our recipes are in the cooking traditions of Mexico, we've incorporated a lot of innovative ingredients. Brie and Mango Quesadillas (page 181) and Cumin-Seared Tofu and Corn Burritos (page 185) suggest the range of delicious innovations.

Any unfamiliar ingredients called for in our recipes, such as nopalitos or chipotle chiles, are available in the ethnic foods section of many large supermarkets. If there's a large Mexican-American community in your city, visit a market in that area of town for a great selection of specialty foods.

Mexican foods are popular with young and old alike. For children or sensitive palates, feel free to reduce the amount of chiles or chili powder called for in the recipes, or eliminate them entirely. Conversely, you may crank up the heat by increasing these fiery seasonings.

MAKE SURE YOUR TORTILLA DISHES ARE CROWD-PLEASERS
BY FOLLOWING THESE TIPS.

For best results, use the freshest tortillas you can find. They should feel soft and pliable in the package. When stale, tortillas become tough and dry and will crack when rolled or folded.

These days, there is a wide array of tortilla choices that go far beyond the white-flour and corn varieties. Whole wheat, sprouted grain, blue corn, and even flavored tortillas are fun to experiment with.

Traditional accompaniments for tortilla dishes include refried beans and Mexican rice, which is typically seasoned with cumin and a bit of tomato. Chips and salsa make a traditional appetizer. (See "Salsa on the Side" on page 173 for more about salsas.)

Most of our tacos are served in soft, heated corn tortillas. If you prefer your tacos crispy, you may substitute ready-made taco shells.

Frequently used seasonings and condiments—such as basil pesto, mayonnaise, and curry powder—are available in all major supermarkets, but they are simple and economical to make at home and keep on hand. See Chapter 2, "Seasonings, Condiments, and Simple Sauces" (page 16), for these useful recipes.

You can easily cook beans, grains, and vegetable stock from scratch. See "Preparing Frequently Used Ingredients" on page 234 to learn how.

Black Bean Tostadas with Avocado and Red Cabbage

These light, yummy morsels offer a great combination of flavors and textures. Purchase crisp tostada shells at any super-market, or make your own by spraying corn tortillas lightly with oil and toasting them directly on the rack in a 400°F (200°C, or gas mark 6) oven until lightly browned and crispy, about 5 minutes per side.

Ingredients

1 can (15 ounces, or 420 g) black beans

1/4 cup (60 g) prepared Salsa Fresca (see recipe, page 26)

2 tablespoons (30 g) plain nonfat yogurt

1 cup (70 g) finely diced red cabbage

2 tablespoons (20 g) finely diced white onion

2 tablespoons (8 g) minced fresh cilantro

1 tablespoon (15 ml) freshly squeezed lime juice

1/2 teaspoon ground cumin

1/4 teaspoon salt

1 medium Haas avocado, diced (see page 240)

4 crisp tostada shells

Place beans in a colander, rinse, and drain. In a bowl, mash the beans with the salsa and yogurt until well combined.

Salsa on the Side

No Mexican meal would be complete without table salsa, as a dip for tortilla chips and for spooning over dishes such as quesadillas, tacos, and burritos. Other tra-ditional condiments for tortilla dishes include sour cream and pickled jalapeno peppers. Although store-bought fresh sal-sas are available, they're easy and fun to make at home, and you can tailor them to your own seasoning preferences. The results are extra special. See Chapter 2, "Seasonings, Condiments, and Simple Sauces," for a few of our favorite recipes:

- Salsa Fresca, page 26
- Smooth Chipotle Chile Salsa, page 27
- Smooth Cilantro Salsa, page 28

In a separate bowl, combine the red cab-bage, onion, cilantro, lime juice, cumin, and salt. Toss to combine well; then add the avocado and toss gently.

Spread beans on tostada shells, top each one with a portion of the cabbage mixture, and serve.

Yield: 4 tostadas

Each will have: 319 calories; 18 g fat; 10 g protein; 39 g carbohydrate; 10 g dietary fiber; trace cholesterol.

Garbanzo, Zucchini, and Olive Tacos with Feta Cheese

Here is a fresh take on tacos, emphasizing Mediterranean instead of Mexican flavors. They are quick and simple to make, light, and refreshing—a great warm-weather meal. If using canned beans, buy two 15-ounce (420-g) cans and measure out the amount needed.

Ingredients

2 cups (350 g) cooked garbanzo beans

2 cups (250 g) diced zucchini

1 cup (160 g) diced white onion

2 cloves garlic, minced

1 teaspoon dried oregano

1 teaspoon dried basil

$1/8$ teaspoon salt

$1/4$ teaspoon coarsely ground black pepper

$1/4$ cup (60 ml) dry white wine

$1/4$ cup (25 g) finely chopped kalamata olives

$1/3$ cup (50 g) crumbled feta cheese

6 taco-size corn tortillas

Place the beans in a colander, rinse, and drain. Combine them in a skillet over medium heat with the zucchini, onion, garlic, oregano, basil, salt, pepper, and wine. Bring to a simmer, cover, and cook for 5 minutes. Stir in the olives and feta.

Just before serving time, wrap the tortillas in a tea towel and heat in a microwave oven until steaming hot, about 1 minute. (Alternatively, you may toast the tortillas one at a time in a hot, dry skillet or over a gas flame, turning frequently.) Place one-sixth of the filling along the center of each tortilla, fold, and serve.

Yield: 6 tacos

Each will have: 191 calories; 5 g fat; 9 g protein; 29 g carbohydrate; 7 g dietary fiber; 8 mg cholesterol.

Spicy Potato and Cauliflower Tacos with Cilantro and Pumpkin Seeds

These unusual tacos were a big hit with our tasters. They do leave a bit of an after-burn, though, so omit the jalapeno pepper or use less than called for if you don't enjoy spicy food.

Ingredients

1 tablespoon (15 ml) canola oil

1/2 onion, finely diced

1/2 pound (225 g) red potatoes, finely diced

2 cups (300 g) finely chopped cauliflower

1 tablespoon dried oregano

1/2 teaspoon salt

1/2 cup (120 ml) vegetable broth or water

1/2 cup (30 g) chopped fresh cilantro

1/4 cup (55 g) raw, unsalted, shelled pumpkin seeds

1 whole pickled jalapeno, stem removed

6 taco-size corn tortillas

Heat the oil in a skillet over medium-high heat. Add the onion, potatoes, cauliflower, oregano, and 1/4 teaspoon of the salt. Sauté, stirring frequently, for 3 minutes. Add the broth, cover, reduce the heat to medium, and cook 5 minutes.

Meanwhile, place the cilantro, pumpkin seeds, pickled jalapeno, remaining 1/4 teaspoon salt, and 1/3 cup (80 ml) of water in the blender. Puree. When the potato-cauliflower cooking time is up, remove the lid and stir in the cilantro mixture.

Just before serving time, wrap the tortillas in a tea towel and heat in a microwave oven until steaming hot, about 1 minute. (Alternatively, you may toast the tortillas one at a time in a hot, dry skillet or over a gas flame, turning frequently.) Place one-sixth of the filling along the center of each tortilla and fold. Serve hot.

Yield: 6 tacos

Each will have: 134 calories; 4 g fat; 4 g protein; 23 g carbohydrate; 4 g dietary fiber; 0 mg cholesterol.

Pinto Bean, Roasted Pepper, and Avocado Tacos

You've heard of taco salad. Now here is a salad taco, with a wonderful combination of veggies and seasonings all wrapped up in a tortilla. These tacos are simple and fresh tasting—a perfect choice for a hot day. Although most of our Mexican-food recipes call for pure chili powder, in this case the standard kind—containing other spices as well as the chili—works best.

Ingredients

1 can (15 ounces, or 420 g) pinto beans

1 tablespoon chili powder

1 cup (180 g) diced roasted red bell pepper

1 cup (120 g) shredded carrots

$^1/_2$ cup (80 g) diced red onion

2 tablespoons (28 ml) freshly squeezed lime juice

$^1/_8$ teaspoon salt

1 medium Haas avocado, diced (see page 240)

6 taco-size corn tortillas

$1^1/_2$ cups (55 g) finely shredded green leaf lettuce

Place the pinto beans in a colander, rinse briefly, and drain well.

Toast the chili powder in a dry, heavy skillet over medium heat, stirring constantly, for 1 minute. Immediately remove it from the pan and set it aside.

In a large bowl, combine the beans, roasted pepper, carrots, onion, lime juice, salt, and toasted chili powder, and toss until well combined. Add the avocado and toss gently so as not to break it up too much.

Just before serving time, wrap the tortillas in a tea towel and heat in a microwave oven until steaming hot, about 1 minute. (Alternatively, you may toast the tortillas one at a time in a hot, dry skillet or over a gas flame, turning frequently.)

Place one-sixth of the filling along the center of each tortilla and fold. Top with a portion of the lettuce and serve.

Yield: 6 tacos
Each will have: 330 calories; 6 g fat; 17 g protein; 55 g carbohydrate; 20 g dietary fiber; 0 mg cholesterol.

Black Bean and Pickled Jalapeno Tacos

Pickled jalapeños are sold in jars or cans and can be found in most supermarkets or any Mexican specialty store. They will keep in the refrigerator for months. Crisp taco shells keep well in the pantry, making this one of those perfect instant meals to invite friends over at the last minute to share.

Ingredients
1 can (15 ounces, or 420 g) black beans
2 tablespoons (18 g) minced pickled jalapeños
$1/4$ teaspoon ground cumin
$1/4$ teaspoon salt
2 fresh pear tomatoes, diced
1 cup (35 g) chopped red leaf lettuce
1 cup (115 g) shredded jack cheese
1 medium Haas avocado, sliced (see page 240)
8 crisp taco shells

Place the beans in a saucepan, along with their liquid. Add the jalapeños, cumin, and salt, and cook over medium-high heat until the liquid is absorbed, about 7 minutes. Stir frequently.

Meanwhile, place the tomato, lettuce, cheese, and avocado on a platter, along with the taco shells, and set out on the table. Offer the beans in a serving bowl and allow diners to assemble their own tacos.

Yield: 8 tacos
Each will have: 335 calories; 10 g fat; 17 g protein; 43 g carbohydrate; 10 g dietary fiber; 14 mg cholesterol.

Mushroom and Cheese Quesadillas

This wonderful mushroom mixture makes a delicious quesadilla. Serve with a selection of table salsas, such as Salsa Fresca (page 26) and Smooth Chipotle Chile Salsa (page 28).

Ingredients

8 ounces (225 g) sliced button mushrooms
1 small white onion, sliced
1 tablespoon (9 g) minced pickled jalapeno pepper
$1/4$ teaspoon ground cumin
$1/4$ teaspoon salt
$1/2$ cup (120 ml) vegetable broth
4 standard-size flour tortillas
1 cup (115 g) shredded mild Cheddar cheese

Place mushrooms, onion, pickled jalapeno, and cumin in a sauté pan. Sprinkle with the salt and pour in the broth. Cover the pan and bring the stock to a rapid simmer over high heat. Uncover the pan, reduce the heat to medium-high, and cook for 8 to 10 minutes, until almost all of the liquid has evaporated.

Meanwhile, heat a large cast-iron skillet or griddle over medium heat. One at a time, place the tortillas in the preheated pan. Place one-fourth of the cheese over half of the tortilla, then top with one-fourth of the mushroom mixture. Fold the tortilla over to enclose the filling. Cook until lightly browned on the bottom, about 2 minutes, then turn and lightly brown the other side. Transfer to a warm platter. Cook the remaining quesadillas in the same fashion. (If you have a large enough skillet, you can cook two at a time.) Cut into wedges and serve.

Yield: 4 quesadillas
Each will have: 377 calories; 15 g fat; 15 g protein; 46 g carbohydrate; 3 g dietary fiber; 30 mg cholesterol.

Quesadillas with Artichoke Pesto and Olive Tapenade

These quesadillas come together quickly with simple ready-made ingredients. Artichoke pesto and olive tapenade are available at specialty markets. The complete-protein sprouted-grain tortillas are a healthier alternative to refined flour varieties.

Ingredients

4 sprouted-grain tortillas

1 cup (112 g) shredded mozzarella cheese

$1/2$ cup (130 g) artichoke pesto

$1/4$ cup (65 g) olive tapenade

One at a time, place the tortillas on a preheated heavy skillet or griddle. Toast for 1 minute, then turn and sprinkle $1/4$ cup (28 g) of the cheese over half the tortilla. Top with 2 tablespoons of the artichoke pesto and 1 tablespoon of the olive tapenade. Fold over to enclose the filling. Cook until lightly browned on the bottom, about 2 minutes, then turn and lightly brown the other side. Transfer to a warm platter. Cook the remaining quesadillas in the same fashion. (If you have a large enough skillet, you can cook two at the same time.) Cut into wedges and serve.

Yield: 4 quesadillas

Each will have: 412 calories; 27 g fat; 15 g protein; 30 g carbohydrate; 2 g dietary fiber; 34 mg cholesterol

Quesadillas with Tequila-Sautéed Peppers and Cheese

This yummy dish is mild by Mexican standards, but if you want it milder still for the sake of the kids, just use plain jack instead of pepper jack cheese. If you don't have a bottle of tequila on hand, you may substitute sherry or white wine.

Ingredients

$1/2$ tablespoon canola oil

2 cups (240 g) finely diced mild fresh peppers, such as red bells or Anaheims

1 onion, finely diced

2 cloves garlic, minced

2 teaspoons ground cumin

1 teaspoon pure chili powder

$1/2$ teaspoon salt

Several grinds black pepper

2 tablespoons (28 ml) tequila

4 standard-size flour tortillas

1 cup (115 g) shredded pepper jack cheese

Heat the oil in a large skillet over medium-high heat. Add the peppers, onion, garlic, cumin, chili powder, salt, and pepper. Sauté, stirring frequently, for 5 minutes. Add the tequila, cover the pan, and cook 2 minutes.

One at a time, place the tortillas on a preheated heavy skillet or griddle. Toast for 1 minute, then turn and spread one-quarter of the pepper mixture over one-half of the tortilla. Top with one-quarter of the cheese and fold over to enclose the filling. Cook until lightly browned on the bottom, about 2 minutes, then turn and lightly brown the other side. Transfer to a warm platter. Cook the remaining quesadillas in the same fashion. (If you have a large enough skillet, you can cook two at the same time.) Cut into wedges and serve.

Yield: 4 quesadillas

Each will have: 409 calories; 16 g fat; 14 g protein; 49 g carbohydrate; 5 g dietary fiber; 25 mg cholesterol.

Brie and Mango Quesadillas

Brie and mango? Yes! This combination of ingredients is a delicious surprise.

Ingredients

1 medium mango

2 green onions

4 standard-size flour tortillas

6 ounces (170 g) brie cheese, thinly sliced

$1/4$ cup (15 g) minced fresh cilantro

$1/4$ cup (60 g) lowfat sour cream

Peel the mango and cut the fruit from the pit, chopping it into small pieces. Set aside. Mince the green onions, discarding the root tips and some of the green portion.

One at a time, place the tortillas on a preheated dry heavy skillet or griddle over medium heat. Top half the tortilla with one-quarter of the cheese, then add $1/4$ of the mango, green onions, and cilantro, and fold over to enclose the filling. Cook until lightly browned on the bottom, about 2 minutes, then turn and lightly brown the other side. Transfer to a warm platter. Cook the remaining quesadillas in the same fashion. (If you have a large enough skillet, you can cook two at a time.) Cut into wedges and serve with 1 tablespoon (15 g) sour cream on top.

Yield: 4 quesadillas

Each will have: 430 calories; 18 g fat; 16 g protein; 51 g carbohydrate; 4 g dietary fiber; 46 mg cholesterol.

Nopalito and Tomato Quesadillas

Nopales—prickly pear cactus paddles—are available fresh year-round in Mexican specialty markets, but they do require laborious preparation. This recipe calls for sliced nopales that are sold in a jar, ready to use, at well-stocked supermarkets and Mexican food stores. Serve with Smooth Cilantro Salsa (page 28) and a dollop of Light Crème Fraîche (page 21) or sour cream. If you can't find queso fresco—fresh Mexican cheese—you may substitute a mild feta.

Ingredients

1 1/4 cups (190 g) sliced *nopales*, chopped

2 fresh pear tomatoes, diced

1 fresh Anaheim chile, seeded and diced

2 green onions

1 tablespoon (15 ml) canola oil

1/2 teaspoon crushed garlic

1/2 teaspoon ground cumin

1/2 teaspoon salt

8 standard-size flour tortillas

1 1/2 cups (225 g) crumbled *queso fresco*

Place the *nopales*, tomatoes, and Anaheim chile in a bowl and toss to combine. Set aside.

Mince the green onions, discarding the root tips and some of the green portion. Place the canola oil in a small skillet and heat over medium-high heat. Stir in the green onions, garlic, and cumin, and sauté for about 1 minute. Add the nopales mixture and the salt. Cook, stirring constantly, until most of the liquid has evaporated, about 4 minutes.

Meanwhile, heat a cast-iron skillet or griddle over medium-high heat. Lay a tortilla in the skillet. Spoon a quarter of the nopalito-and-tomato mixture on top, creating an even layer. Sprinkle with one-quarter of the cheese and place another tortilla on top. Cook for about 3 minutes, then flip the quesadilla and continue to cook for 2 to 3 minutes, until lightly browned. Transfer to a warm platter. Cook the remaining quesadillas in the same manner. Cut into wedges and serve.

Yield: 4 quesadillas

Each will have: 516 calories; 22 g fat; 18 g protein; 62 g carbohydrate; 5 g dietary fiber; 50 mg cholesterol.

Burritos with Spinach, Artichokes, Roasted Peppers, and Feta Cheese

This Mediterranean take on the burrito is assembled at the table and does not need any condiments.

Ingredients

1 cup (160 g) cooked basmati rice

1/4 cup (15 g) minced fresh parsley

2 tablespoons (28 ml) extra-virgin olive oil

10 ounces (280 g) washed fresh spinach leaves, chopped

1 jar (6 ounces, or 170 g) marinated artichoke hearts

1/2 cup (90 g) chopped roasted red bell pepper

1 tablespoon dried marjoram

6 burrito-size flour tortillas

1 1/2 cups (225 g) crumbled feta cheese

Place the rice in a bowl along with the parsley and 1 tablespoon (15 ml) of the olive oil. Set aside.

Pile the spinach in a skillet that has a tight-fitting lid. Add 1/4 cup (60 ml) water, cover, and cook over medium heat until spinach wilts, about 3 to 4 minutes. Meanwhile, drain the artichoke hearts and chop them finely.

Transfer the cooked spinach to a colander and press with a wooden spoon or squeeze with your hands to remove the excess water. Return the spinach to the skillet and add the artichoke hearts, red bell pepper, marjoram, and rice mixture. Cook over medium-high heat for 2 to 3 minutes, stirring well to combine.

Transfer the skillet to the table, placing it on a trivet or other hot-pan holder. Toast the tortillas briefly in a skillet and bring them to the table. Invite diners to evenly spoon the spinach mixture onto a tortilla, adding feta cheese to taste, and roll tightly to enclose the filling.

Yield: 6 burritos

Each will have: 446 calories; 20 g fat; 14 g protein; 53 g carbohydrate; 5 g dietary fiber; 33 mg cholesterol

Sprouted Grain and Spicy Refried Bean Burritos

These burritos use a sprouted-grain tortilla that is more nutritious than the refined-flour variety. You can buy spicy jalapeno refried beans ready-made in cans at the supermarket, or substitute the black bean and pickled jalapeno filling from our Black Bean and Pickled Jalapeno Tacos recipe on page 177. If fresh watercress is not in season, simply delete it or use fresh cilantro.

Ingredients

4 sprouted-grain tortillas

1 cup (250 g) spicy jalapeno refried beans

$1/2$ cup (60 g) diced yellow bell pepper

$1/2$ cup (60 g) crumbled fresh goat cheese (chevre)

$1/4$ cup (15 g) watercress leaves

Zest of 2 medium limes

Place the tortillas on the countertop and mound $1/4$ of the refried beans in the center of each tortilla. Add $1/4$ of the yellow bell pepper, goat cheese, and watercress. Sprinkle with a portion of the lime zest, fold in one side of the tortilla, and roll tightly to enclose the filling. Place seam-side down on a plate and microwave on high for 3 minutes.

Yield: 4 burritos

Each will have: 261 calories; 9 g fat; 12 g protein; 37 g carbohydrate; 5 g dietary fiber; 15 mg cholesterol.

Cumin-Seared Tofu and Corn Burritos

Here is a simple and delicious combination that can be enjoyed immediately but also travels well. Simply wrap each burrito tightly in plastic wrap or aluminum foil and pack for a workday lunch or a picnic in the park. If you can't find spinach tortillas, substitute another variety.

Ingredients

1 pound (455 g) firm tofu

1 tablespoon (15 ml) canola oil

1 medium yellow onion, diced

1 tablespoon ground cumin

1/4 teaspoon cayenne pepper

3/4 teaspoon salt

1 1/2 cups (240 g) frozen corn
   kernels

4 cloves garlic, minced

1/3 cup (80 g) plain nonfat yogurt

1/3 cup (80 g) lowfat sour cream

1/3 cup (20 g) minced fresh
   cilantro

6 burrito-size spinach tortillas

1 1/2 cups (55 g) shredded red
   leaf lettuce

Dice the tofu into 1/2-inch (1.25-cm) cubes. Heat the oil in a skillet over medium-high heat and add the onion and cumin. Sauté for 1 minute, then add the tofu, cayenne, and 1/2 teaspoon of the salt. Cook, stirring occasionally, for 3 minutes, then add the corn, garlic, and water. Cook, stirring occasionally, for 5 minutes longer.

Meanwhile, combine the yogurt, sour cream, and cilantro in a bowl, along with the remaining 1/4 teaspoon salt. Stir until well blended and set aside. When the tofu is done, turn off the heat and stir in the yogurt mixture.

Just before serving, wrap the tortillas in a tea towel and heat in a microwave oven until steaming hot, about 1 minute. (For a crispier texture, heat the tortillas one at a time in a dry, heavy skillet or griddle, turning once or twice until browned.)

Place one-sixth of the tofu mixture along the center of each tortilla. Top with a portion of the lettuce, then fold in the bottom and sides and roll up tightly to enclose the filling.

Yield: 6 burritos
Each will have: 388 calories; 12 g fat; 16 g protein; 57 g carbohydrate; 4 g dietary fiber; 3 mg cholesterol.

CHAPTER TWELVE

15-MINUTE
GRILLED AND
BROILED DISHES

In the age of instant-on outdoor gas grills and stovetop or countertop models for indoors, grilling has become an ever more popular and convenient cooking method. Likewise, the broiler in your conventional oven or toaster oven heats up quickly and can make fast work of meal preparation.

We have used these high-heat cooking methods to create an interesting variety of dishes, from simple sides like Grilled Sweet Potatoes (page 189) to innovative main courses like Curry-Broiled Tempeh with Pineapple Raita (pages 202–203). Our other offerings include pizzas, frittatas, and stuffed vegetables. The pizzas rely on ready-made, precooked crusts—another great convenience food—which require only a few minutes of cooking once the toppings are added. For the highest nutrient values, look for a whole-grain variety at a natural food store.

In the warm-weather months, cooking outdoors on a gas grill is casual, convenient, and carefree—if you heed a few simple precautions (see "Pointers from the Pros" on page 188). Many a great garden party at our homes has centered around this type of cooking. See "Cooking Al Fresco" on page 189 for a special midsummer menu plan.

Let the recipes in this chapter inspire your own grilling and broiling adventures!

FOLLOW THESE TIPS TO MAKE SURE YOUR GRILLING ADVENTURES ARE SAFE, DELICIOUS, AND FUN.

An outdoor gas, stovetop, or countertop grill takes no more than 5 minutes to preheat.

Spray or brush the grill lightly with oil just before placing the food on to cook.

Utilize a wire brush to clean the grill after every use, removing any charred bits of food that are stuck to the grate.

Set up the grill in a well-ventilated area so you're not breathing in smoke as you cook.

To prevent burns, use long-handled tongs and spatulas when cooking on an outdoor grill.

Take care to prevent fires by placing the grill well away from combustible items, not wearing flowing garments, and not grilling on an extremely windy day.

Most of our broiled recipes call for foods to be cooked 4 to 6 inches (10 to 15 cm) from the heat source. If your oven has a broiler on the top, adjust the upper rack accordingly. If your broiler is in a separate drawer on the bottom of the oven, you may be cooking the food a bit closer to the heat source. Check broiling foods frequently so they don't scorch on the top.

Frequently used seasonings and condiments—such as basil pesto, mayonnaise, and curry powder—are available in all major supermarkets, but they are simple and economical to make at home and keep on hand. See Chapter 2, "Seasonings, Condiments, and Simple Sauces" (page 16), for these useful recipes.

You can easily cook beans, grains, and vegetable stock from scratch. See "Preparing Frequently Used Ingredients" on page 234 to learn how.

Grilled Sweet Potatoes

This is a wonderful way to serve red sweet potatoes, which are sometimes sold as yams. Other potatoes, such as red, russet, or Yukon Gold, also are delicious when grilled this way. Top the slices with small dollops of sour cream, if you wish.

Ingredients

4 medium (1^1/$_2$ lbs.) red-skinned sweet
    potatoes
2 tablespoons (28 ml) extra-virgin olive oil
^{1}/$_2$ teaspoon granulated garlic
^{1}/$_8$ teaspoon salt

Preheat the grill to medium-high. Scrub the sweet potatoes but do not peel them. Slice them crosswise into ^{1}/$_2$-inch (1.25-cm) rounds. Place the slices in a plastic bag and drizzle with the olive oil, then sprinkle in the garlic and salt. Twist the bag to seal, allowing some air to remain in the bag. Gently toss the sweet potato slices with the oil and seasonings until they are evenly coated. Transfer them to the grill, and grill for 10 to 12 minutes, turning frequently, until they are fork-tender and showing grill marks.

Yield: 6 servings

Each will have: 132 calories; 5 g fat; 1 g protein; 21 g carbohydrate; 3 g dietary fiber; 0 mg cholesterol.

Cooking Al Fresco

This midsummer party idea is simplicity itself. Prepare the appetizer, salad dressing, and dessert in advance, then relax on the patio with your guests when they arrive. Serve mineral water or your favorite vintage of wine with the artichoke spread, then fire up the grill when you're ready to finish preparing the meal. A few minutes before serving time, ask a friend to mind the grill while you dash inside to whip up the couscous. Bon appetit!

Here's what to serve:

- Artichoke and Parmesan Spread with baguette slices (page 54)

- Savory Grilled Tofu (page 199)

- Grilled Eggplant with Pesto and Red Bell Peppers (page 190)

- Couscous with Feta, Olives, and Walnuts (page 152)

- Mixed greens with Meyer Lemon Vinaigrette (page 69)

- Ricotta Cheese "Fluff" with Raspberry Sauce and Chocolate Shavings (page 225)

Grilled Eggplant with Pesto and Red Bell Peppers

Eggplant grills quickly and makes a perfect base for colorful toppings such as green pesto and bright red peppers. You may serve this as a side dish or an appetizer.

Ingredients

1 medium eggplant
2 tablespoons (28 ml) extra-virgin olive oil
$1/2$ teaspoon granulated garlic
$1/4$ cup (65 g) Basil Pesto (see recipe, page 23)
$1/2$ cup (90 g) chopped roasted red bell peppers

Preheat the grill to medium-high. Cut the eggplant crosswise into slices about $1/2$-inch (1.25-cm) thick. Place the slices in a plastic bag, drizzle in the olive oil, and sprinkle in the granulated garlic. Twist the bag to close, allowing some air to remain in the bag. Gently toss the eggplant with the oil and garlic until it is evenly coated. Transfer the eggplant slices to the grill, and grill until lightly browned on one side, about 3 to 4 minutes. Turn, and cook an additional 3 to 4 minutes to lightly brown the other side.

Meanwhile, place the pesto in a glass measuring cup and stir in 1 tablespoon (15 ml) of water. Microwave the pesto on high for 30 seconds. When the eggplant is done, place the slices on a warm platter or individual serving plates. Drizzle or spoon the pesto over the eggplant and top evenly with the roasted peppers.

Yield: 4 servings

Each will have: 169 calories; 14 g fat; 4 g protein; 9 g carbohydrate; 3 g dietary fiber; 4mg cholesterol.

Broiled Eggplant
with Dried Tomato Marinara

You could also use this delicious and simple marinara sauce on pasta or as a pizza topping.

Ingredients

$1/2$ teaspoon canola oil

1 medium globe eggplant (about $1^{1}/_{4}$ pounds, or 560 g)

$1/2$ teaspoon salt

$1/2$ teaspoon pepper

1 cup (240 g) diced canned tomatoes, undrained

$1/3$ cup (35 g) oil-packed dried tomatoes, drained

1 clove garlic, chopped

1 tablespoon dried oregano

$1/4$ cup (25 g) grated Parmesan or Romano cheese (or a blend)

Preheat the broiler. Lightly oil a baking sheet and set aside.

Cut the eggplant crosswise into $1/2$-inch (1.25-cm) slices, discarding the ends. Arrange the slices on the baking sheet and season them with $1/4$ teaspoon of the salt and $1/4$ teaspoon of the pepper. Broil 4 inches (10 cm) from the heat source until lightly browned, about 6 minutes, then turn and broil 3 minutes longer, until softened and lightly browned.

Meanwhile, in a blender or food processor, combine the canned tomatoes, dried tomatoes, garlic, oregano, remaining $1/4$ teaspoon salt and $1/4$ teaspoon pepper. Puree.

When the eggplant is done, top each slice with a dollop of the sauce and spread it out to cover the eggplant evenly. Top with a portion of the cheese and return to the broiler for 1 minute.

Yield: 4 servings

Each will have: 97 calories; 4 g fat; 5 g protein; 13 g carbohydrate; 5 g dietary fiber; 4mg cholesterol.

Peppers Stuffed with Wild Rice and Mozzarella

This makes a wonderful light lunch entrée or special supper side dish.

Ingredients

3 large red or yellow bell peppers

$1^1/_2$ cups (250 g) cooked wild rice

1 cup (112 g) shredded mozzarella

$^1/_4$ cup (15 g) minced fresh parsley

2 tablespoons (28 ml) white wine

1 tablespoon (15 ml) extra-virgin olive oil

1 tablespoon Italian herb seasoning

2 teaspoons crushed garlic

$^1/_2$ teaspoon salt

$^1/_4$ teaspoon coarsely ground black pepper

Preheat the broiler. Cut each bell pepper in half from top to bottom and remove the stems, seeds, and thick white membranes. Cut each pepper-half in half to create 4 boat-shaped quarters. Set aside.

In a bowl, combine the wild rice, mozzarella, parsley, wine, olive oil, Italian seasoning, garlic, salt, and pepper. Mix well. Fill the pepper "boats" with the rice mixture, pressing it firmly into place. Arrange the peppers stuffing-side up on a baking sheet and broil 4 inches (10 cm) from the heat source until the cheese is melted and lightly browned, about 5 minutes.

Yield: 6 servings

Each will have: 143 calories; 7 g fat; 6 g protein; 14 g carbohydrate; 2 g dietary fiber; 17 mg cholesterol.

Zucchini Stuffed with Pesto and Ricotta Cheese

This zucchini has a slight crunch that provides a lovely counterpoint to the soft and fluffy filling. It's a delicious side dish!

Ingredients

4 medium zucchini

1/2 cup (125 g) lowfat ricotta cheese

1/4 cup (65 g) Basil Pesto (see recipe, page 23)

1 tablespoon (15 ml) freshly squeezed lemon juice

Preheat the broiler. Slice the zucchini in half, discarding the stem ends. Use a melon baller or spoon to scoop out and discard the seeds to create 8 hollow "boats." If the halves will not sit flat, trim a bit off the bottom, but be careful not to cut all the way through. Place the zucchini boats in a shallow dish with a bit of water, and cook in the microwave oven until just fork-tender, about 3 minutes.

Meanwhile, place the ricotta cheese in a bowl and stir in the pesto and lemon juice.

Remove the zucchini from the microwave oven. Place the zucchini boats on paper towels for a moment to drain off any excess water. Transfer them to a baking sheet and spoon equal amounts of the ricotta mixture into them, spreading it out to evenly coat the hollowed-out area. Broil 4 inches (10 cm) from the heat source until bubbly and slightly browned, about 2 minutes.

Yield: 8 servings
Each will have: 74 calories; 5 g fat; 4 g protein; 4 g carbohydrate; 1 g dietary fiber; 7 mg cholesterol.

Portobello Mushrooms Stuffed with Savory Bread Crumbs

These scrumptious mushrooms are a winner every time. Portobello mushrooms can range in size from about 2 to 4 inches (5 to 10 cm) across. Use medium-sized ones for this dish.

Ingredients

1 tablespoon (15 ml) extra-virgin olive oil
4 medium portobello mushrooms
4 green onions
1 cup (110 g) fine plain bread crumbs
$1/3$ cup (80 ml) vegetable broth
$1/4$ cup (60 ml) dry white wine
$1/4$ cup (25 g) grated Parmesan cheese
1 tablespoon dried basil
$1/4$ teaspoon salt
Several grinds black pepper

Preheat the broiler. Use 1 teaspoon of the olive oil to lightly rub the mushroom caps. Place them cap-side-up on a baking sheet and broil 4 inches (10 cm) from the heat source until browning nicely, about 5 minutes.

Meanwhile, mince the green onions, discarding the root tips and some of the green portion. Combine the bread crumbs with the remaining olive oil, green onions, broth, wine, Parmesan, basil, salt, and pepper. Mix well.

Remove the portobellos from the oven and flip them over. Mound one-quarter of the bread crumb mixture on each mushroom, pressing down firmly. Broil, filling-side-up, until lightly browned, about 3 minutes.

Yield: 4 servings
Each will have: 218 calories; 7 g fat; 9 g protein; 29 g carbohydrate; 3 g dietary fiber; 4 mg cholesterol.

Grilled Pizza with Artichokes, Cheese, and Olives

These ingredients suggest a Greek theme. If you can't find the roasted garlic tomato sauce at your market, you may substitute 1 cup (250 g) of your favorite tomato marinara sauce. Complete the meal with a mixed green salad tossed with Tomato Balsamic Vinaigrette (page 20) and garnished with cooked garbanzo beans.

Ingredients

1 prebaked 12-inch (30-cm) pizza crust

1 can (8 ounces, or 225 g) roasted garlic tomato sauce

1 cup (112 g) shredded mozzarella cheese

1 jar (6 ounces, or 170 g) marinated artichoke hearts, drained and chopped

1 cup (150 g) crumbled feta cheese

$1/4$ cup (25 g) pitted and chopped kalamata olives

Preheat a gas grill to high. Place the pizza crust on a pizza stone and spread the tomato sauce evenly over it, leaving about a 1-inch (2.5-cm) border all the way around free of sauce. Top the sauce with the mozzarella cheese, then the artichoke hearts. Sprinkle on the feta cheese and kalamata olives. Transfer to the grill, cover, and cook until the cheese has melted, about 10 minutes. Remove from the grill, cut into 8 slices, and serve.

Yield: 8 slices

Each will have: 291 calories; 12 g fat; 12 g protein; 35 g carbohydrate; 2 g dietary fiber; 30 mg cholesterol.

Grilled Pizza with Ricotta and Fresh Greens

This is pizza and salad, all rolled into one. Serve it with white wine for a lovely meal with friends.

Ingredients

1 prebaked 12-inch (30-cm) pizza crust

$^1/_4$ cup (65 g) tomato marinara sauce

2 tablespoons (10 g) grated Parmesan cheese

$^1/_4$ cup (25 g) sliced kalamata olives

$^1/_2$ cup (125 g) lowfat ricotta cheese

2 tablespoons (30 g) lowfat sour cream

1 teaspoon dried oregano

1 tablespoon (15 ml) extra-virgin olive oil

1 teaspoon freshly squeezed lemon juice

Pinch of salt

Several grinds black pepper

2 cups (40 g) prewashed mixed salad greens

Preheat a gas grill to high. Place the crust on a pizza stone and spread the tomato sauce over the top to evenly cover the crust, all the way to the outside edge. Sprinkle the Parmesan cheese evenly over the sauce, then distribute the olives over the cheese.

In a small bowl, combine the ricotta cheese, sour cream, and oregano. Place 8 heaping teaspoons of the cheese mixture on the pizza, evenly spaced around the outer edge. Transfer the pizza to a hot grill and cover the grill. Cook until hot and the cheese has softened a bit, about 10 minutes.

Meanwhile, whisk together the oil, lemon juice, salt, and pepper. Place the greens in a bowl and toss with the dressing. Remove the pizza from the grill and cut into 8 slices. Mound the greens in the center of the pizza and serve.

Yield: 8 slices

Each will have: 224 calories; 7 g fat; 8 g protein; 33 g carbohydrate; 1 g dietary fiber; 7 mg cholesterol.

Pizza with Sautéed Mushrooms, Mozzarella, and Fresh Herbs

Most of the time here is spent finely chopping the mixed herbs, which can be done while the mushrooms are cooking. You'll have a delicious "gourmet" pizza on the table in no time! For the fresh herbs, use any combination of parsley, basil, rosemary, and/or oregano.

Ingredients

1 tablespoon (15 ml) extra-virgin olive oil
12 ounces (340 g) sliced button mushrooms
2 teaspoons crushed garlic
$1/4$ teaspoon salt
Several grinds black pepper
2 tablespoons (28 ml) dry sherry or white wine
1 prebaked 12-inch (30-cm) pizza crust
$1^1/2$ cups (170 g) shredded mozzarella cheese
$1/4$ cup (15 g) minced fresh herbs

Preheat the broiler. Heat the oil in a sauté pan over medium-high heat. Add the mushrooms, garlic, salt, and pepper, and sauté until the mushrooms release their liquid and most of it has evaporated, about 4 minutes. Add the sherry, and stir and sauté 2 minutes longer.

Spread the mushrooms over the pizza crust, leaving a 1-inch (2.5-cm) border all the way around free of topping. Distribute the cheese evenly over the mushrooms, then sprinkle on the fresh herbs. Broil 4 inches (10 cm) from the heat source until the cheese is bubbly, about 3 minutes. Remove from the broiler and cut into 8 slices and serve.

Yield: 8 slices
Each will have: 264 calories; 10 g fat; 11 g protein; 33 g carbohydrate; 1 g dietary fiber; 19 mg cholesterol.

Pizza with Pesto, Fresh Tomatoes, and Parmesan

If you use a store-bought pesto for this recipe rather than making it from scratch, read the label and make sure it is made with basil and olive oil, not other herbs and oils. This will ensure a delicious depth of flavor.

Ingredients

1 clove garlic, minced
$^1/_2$ cup (125 g) Basil Pesto (see recipe, page 23)
1 prebaked 12-inch (30-cm) pizza crust
1 medium tomato, thinly sliced
$^1/_4$ cup (25 g) grated Parmesan cheese

Preheat the broiler. Stir the garlic into the pesto and spread the pesto on the crust, leaving about a 1-inch (2.5-cm) margin all the way around free of pesto. Arrange tomato slices on the pizza in a single layer. Top evenly with the cheese and broil 4 inches (10 cm) from the heat source until bubbly, about 3 minutes. Remove from the broiler and cut into 8 slices and serve.

Yield: 8 slices
Each will have: 255 calories; 10 g fat; 9 g protein; 32 g carbohydrate; 1 g dietary fiber; 7 mg cholesterol.

Tofu and Spinach English Muffin "Pizzas"

This is a great recipe to cook with kids. The tasks are simple and fun for little hands to help with, and the results are mild and yummy. Even grown-ups like 'em! The recipe makes 8 servings for small appetites, 4 servings for bigger ones.

Ingredients

4 ounces (115 g) frozen chopped spinach
8 ounces (225 g) firm tofu
1 cup (250 g) tomato marinara sauce
2 tablespoons (10 g) grated Parmesan cheese
4 English muffins, halved and toasted
1 cup (112 g) shredded mozzarella cheese

Preheat the broiler. Thaw the spinach by placing it in a strainer and rinsing with warm water until it is soft. Press with a wooden spoon or squeeze gently with your hands to remove excess water. Transfer the spinach to a bowl. Crumble the tofu into the bowl and add the marinara sauce and Parmesan. Stir to combine well.

Mound equal amounts of the tofu mixture on the toasted English muffin halves and top with equal amounts of the mozzarella. Broil about 4 inches (10 cm) from the heat source until the cheese is bubbly and lightly browned, about 3 minutes.

Yield: 8 "pizzas"
Each will have: 161 calories; 6 g fat; 9 g protein; 17 g carbohydrate; 2 g dietary fiber; 14 mg cholesterol.

VEGAN

Savory Grilled Tofu

Grilling tofu that has been liberally seasoned creates a delicious depth of flavor. Serve these tasty morsels to boost the protein quotient of any meal.

Ingredients

1 pound (455 g) extra-firm tofu

3 tablespoons (45 ml) extra-virgin olive oil

1 tablespoon (15 ml) balsamic vinegar

1 tablespoon (15 ml) soy sauce

1 teaspoon crushed garlic

1 teaspoon paprika

Several grinds black pepper

Preheat the grill to medium.

Pat the tofu dry with paper towels to remove any surface moisture. Cut the tofu into 4 equal-sized pieces that are about 1 inch (2.5 cm) thick. In a glass baking dish, whisk together the oil, vinegar, soy sauce, garlic, paprika, and pepper. Add the tofu, and use your hands to distribute the marinade evenly over all the pieces, rubbing it in well but being careful not to break up the tofu.

Transfer the tofu to the grill and grill for about 10 minutes, turning several times, until it is nicely browned. Transfer to a platter and serve.

Yield: 4 servings

Each will have: 204 calories; 17 g fat; 12 g protein; 3 g carbohydrate; 1 g dietary fiber; 0 mg cholesterol.

Broiled Frittata with Potato Chips and Jalapeños

Serve this frittata as an appetizer, lunch, or even a breakfast dish with fresh fruit. Served with a salad, bread, and cheese, it becomes an intimate dinner for two.

Ingredients

4 large eggs

2 ounces (55 g) potato chips, coarsely crushed (about 2 cups)

2 tablespoons (14 g) minced oil-packed dried tomatoes

1 jalapeno pepper, seeded and minced

1 teaspoon extra-virgin olive oil

2 tablespoons (30 g) lowfat sour cream

Preheat the broiler, with the rack about 8 inches (20 cm) from the heat source. Place the eggs in a bowl and beat them until fluffy. Transfer half of the eggs into another bowl and add the potato chips. Set aside for 2 minutes so the potato chips can soften slightly. Stir in the reserved eggs, dried tomatoes, and jalapeno pepper.

In a 10-inch (25-cm) cast-iron or nonstick ovenproof skillet, heat the olive oil over medium heat. When the oil is hot, add the egg mixture and cook until the bottom is set and golden brown, about 2 to 3 minutes (use a spatula to gently lift the eggs away from the bottom of the pan to check). Transfer the skillet to the broiler and broil for 1 to 2 minutes, until the top is set and golden brown. Check after about 1 minute to make sure it doesn't scorch on top. Cut into quarters and serve with a dollop of the sour cream on each quarter.

Yield: 4 servings

Each will have: 184 calories; 13 g fat; 8 g protein; 9 g carbohydrate; 1 g dietary fiber; 215 mg cholesterol.

Broiled Frittata with Mozzarella Cheese and Roasted Red Bell Peppers

For a simple yet special supper, serve this delicious frittata with steamed asparagus, a hearty salad, and crusty whole-grain bread.

Ingredients

4 large eggs

1 cup (150 g) grated mozzarella cheese

$1/4$ cup (45 g) chopped roasted red bell pepper

1 tablespoon (15 ml) extra-virgin olive oil

Preheat the broiler with the rack about 8 inches (20 cm) from the heat source. Place the eggs in a bowl and beat them until fluffy. Stir in the cheese and roasted red bell pepper.

In a 10-inch (25-cm) cast-iron or nonstick ovenproof skillet, heat the olive oil over medium heat. When the oil is hot, add the egg mixture and cook until the bottom is set and golden brown, about 2 to 3 minutes (use a spatula to gently lift the eggs away from the bottom of the pan to check). Transfer the skillet to the broiler, and broil for 1 to 2 minutes, until the top is set and golden brown. Check after about 1 minute to make sure it doesn't scorch on top. Cut into quarters and serve on warm plates.

Yield: 4 servings

Each will have: 196 calories; 15 g fat; 12 g protein; 1 g carbohydrate; trace dietary fiber; 237 mg cholesterol.

Curry-Broiled Tempeh with Pineapple Raita

Raita is a refreshing Indian yogurt-based condiment that helps cool down the fire of spicy food. This recipe pairs perfectly with Basmati Rice with Saffron and Cumin Seeds (page 157). A simple steamed vegetable or leafy salad would round out the meal nicely.

Ingredients

1 tablespoon (15 ml) dark sesame oil

1 tablespoon (15 ml) freshly squeezed lime juice

$1/2$ tablespoon soy sauce

$1/2$ tablespoon mild curry powder

1 teaspoon crushed garlic

$1/4$ teaspoon salt

2 tablespoons (28 ml) pineapple juice (from canned pineapple)

12 ounces (340 g) soy tempeh

$1/2$ cup (125 g) plain nonfat yogurt

2 tablespoons (8 g) minced fresh mint leaves

$1/2$ teaspoon ground cumin

Several grinds black pepper

$2/3$ cup (135 g) canned crushed pineapple, drained (juice reserved)

Preheat the broiler.

In a large bowl, whisk together the oil, lime juice, soy sauce, curry powder, garlic, $1/8$ teaspoon of the salt, and the 2 tablespoons (28 ml) of pineapple juice. Cut the tempeh slabs crosswise into $1/2$-inch (1.25-cm) strips about 3 inches (7.5 cm) in length. Add the tempeh to the bowl and use your hands to toss and rub the seasoning mixture evenly into the tempeh strips.

Transfer the tempeh to a baking sheet in a single layer and broil 4 inches (10 cm) from the heat source until browning nicely, about 2 to 3 minutes. Turn and broil for 2 to 3 more minutes.

Meanwhile, stir together the yogurt, mint, cumin, remaining $1/8$ teaspoon salt, and pepper, then add the pineapple and stir to combine. Arrange the tempeh strips in a haystack shape on each plate, with a spoonful of the pineapple raita spooned over the top.

Yield: 4 servings
Each will have: 253 calories; 10 g fat; 18 g protein; 26 g carbohydrate; 1 g dietary fiber; 1 mg cholesterol.

CHAPTER THIRTEEN

15-MINUTE BEVERAGES

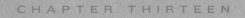

Plain, filtered water is the elixir of health, but there are moments that call for something yummy in our glasses and cups. In this chapter we offer a tasty selection of hot and cold drinks to suit many moods and occasions.

Hot beverages like Orange Spice Hot Chocolate (page 216) and Honey-Streaked Latte (page 213) are perfect lazy-morning comfort drinks. Curl up with a good book, magazine, or newspaper and enjoy! Hot summer days, on the other hand, call for refreshing drinks like Lavender Lemonade (page 208) and Sangria (page 210), a fruit juice and red wine concoction that hails from Spain and is a wonderful accompaniment to hot and spicy foods.

If you have room in your freezer, keep several tall beverage glasses there, ready to use for chilled drinks. When serving hot beverages, it's worth the minor effort to warm the brandy snifters, mugs, or coffee cups you'll be using by filling them with hot water and setting them aside while you prepare the beverage.

This chapter carries one caveat: Though all of our beverage recipes are quick and simple to make, some are not quite ready to drink in 15 minutes. When steeped or brewed beverages, such as tea or coffee, are to be served cold, plan on about 30 minutes of chilling time in the refrigerator. If you pour them over ice when steaming hot, the ice will melt instantly and dilute the flavor of the beverage. Of course, you could also prepare such beverages up to a day or two ahead of serving time.

Whether hot or cold, once you've tried our special beverages you'll find yourself returning to them again and again.

TRY THESE TIPS FOR PERFECT DRINKS EVERY TIME.

Use pure, filtered water, not tap water, for all your beverages. It tastes better, and it's better for your health.

Green and black teas are being touted for their antioxidant powers and are healthful additions to the diet.

When brewed tea or coffee beverages are to be served cold, allow them to cool to room temperature or chill them in the refrigerator before pouring them over ice. This prevents the ice from diluting the flavor of the beverage.

For our coffee drinks, we always buy whole beans and grind them as needed. Preground coffee can oxidize rapidly, losing its robust character and developing off flavors.

Where coffee or tea is called for in these recipes, you may use the decaffeinated variety if you want a nonstimulating beverage.

 VEGAN

Orange Ginger Cooler

This very refreshing beverage could include a shot of tequila, if you wish.

Ingredients
1 tablespoon grated fresh ginger
2 tablespoons (40 g) honey
1 quart (9464 ml) sparkling mineral water
1 cup (235 ml) freshly squeezed orange juice
2 tablespoons (28 ml) freshly squeezed lime juice

Place the ginger and honey in a bowl and cover with 1 cup (235 ml) boiling water. Set aside to steep for at least 5 minutes. In a pitcher, combine the mineral water with the orange juice and lime juice. When the ginger has finished steeping, strain the liquid into the pitcher. Stir to combine and serve over ice.

Yield: 4 servings
Each will have: 63 calories; trace fat; 1 g protein; 16 g carbohydrate; trace dietary fiber; 0 mg cholesterol.

Melon and Mint Cooler

This frothy beverage delivers the flavor, fiber, and antioxidant power of cantaloupe, enlivened by mint and citrus juice. Refrigerate the melon ahead of time so you won't need to add ice, which dilutes the flavor.

Ingredients

1 medium chilled cantaloupe

1/2 cup (120 ml) freshly squeezed orange juice

1/4 cup (15 g) fresh mint, chopped

2 tablespoons (28 ml) freshly squeezed lime juice

4 mint sprigs

Cut the cantaloupe in half and use a spoon to scoop out and discard the seeds. Cut chunks of cantaloupe out of the skin and place them in the blender with the orange juice, mint, and lime juice. Pulse to puree. Pour into tall beverage glasses and garnish each serving with a mint sprig.

Yield: 4 servings

Each will have: 67 calories; trace fat; 2 g protein; 16 g carbohydrate; 2 g dietary fiber; 0 mg cholesterol.

Gifts of the Vine

Yes, wine belongs on the vegetarian table! A good wine has subtle flavor nuances that can enhance our enjoyment of fine foods. When selecting a wine to pair with the evening meal, keep in mind that deep savory flavors are generally complemented by red wines, while creamy or delicately seasoned dishes call for a white varietal. We usually prefer dry white and red wines; however, a fruity white with a crisp finish is the perfect beverage to serve with hot and spicy foods. Drinking wine may even offer health benefits. It stimulates digestion, provides a dose of antioxidants, helps us relax and enjoy our meals, and can promote heart health when consumed in moderation.

Lavender Lemonade

Culinary lavender adds an intriguing flavor note to Herbes de Provence (page 29), and it's also great for making tea. Here, lavender tea becomes the base for a distinctive lemonade, which starts out light bronze in color but turns a lovely shade of pink when the lemon juice is added. Garnish the glasses with fresh sprigs of lavender, if you have some on hand. (Note that this beverage requires at least 30 minutes of chilling time after the quick preparation—or it can be made up to a day or two in advance.)

Ingredients

3 tablespoons (15 g) dried lavender flowers
$1/4$ cup (60 ml) freshly squeezed lemon
   juice
2 tablespoons (25 g) granulated sugar

Place the lavender flowers in a teapot or glass or ceramic bowl and cover with 4 cups (.95 L) of boiling water. Set aside to steep for 10 minutes, then strain into a pitcher and add the lemon juice and sugar. Stir until the sugar dissolves, and then refrigerate. When cool, serve over ice in 4 tall glasses.

Yield: 4 servings

Each will have: 28 calories; 0 g fat; trace protein; 8 g carbohydrate; trace dietary fiber; 0 mg cholesterol.

Iced Tea with Raspberry Syrup

Enlivening iced tea with a splash of fruit syrup—the kind used to make Italian sodas—brings it to a whole new level. Offer this at your next al fresco lunch or brunch gathering. (Note that this beverage requires at least 30 minutes of chilling time after the quick preparation—or it can be made up to a day or two in advance.)

Ingredients

4 black tea bags
$1/4$ cup (60 ml) raspberry syrup
   (such as Torani)
4 lemon wedges

Place the tea bags in a teapot or pitcher and pour 6 cups (1.4 L) boiling water over them. Steep for 5 minutes, then discard the tea bags and refrigerate the tea. When cool, serve over ice in 4 tall glasses. Pour 1 tablespoon (15 ml) of the syrup into each glass, garnish with a lemon wedge, and serve.

Yield: 4 servings

Each will have: 63 calories; 0 g fat; trace protein; 17 g carbohydrate; trace dietary fiber; 0 mg cholesterol.

Iced Green Tea with Mandarin Oranges

Here is a green tea beverage that highlights a traditional flavor of the Far East, mandarin oranges. Buy an 11-ounce (312 g) can; you will need some of the segments and most of the syrup. (Note that this beverage requires at least 30 minutes of chilling time after the quick preparation—or it can be made up to a day or two in advance.)

Ingredients

4 green tea bags

12 segments canned mandarin oranges in
   light syrup

$^1/_4$ cup (60 ml) mandarin orange syrup
   (from can)

Ground nutmeg for garnish

Place the tea bags in a teapot or pitcher and pour 4 cups (.95 L) boiling water over them. Steep for 5 minutes, then discard the tea bags and refrigerate the tea. When it has cooled off, stir in the oranges and syrup and pour over ice in 4 tall glasses, dusting each serving with just a bit of ground nutmeg.

Yield: 4 servings

Each will have: 20 calories; trace fat; trace protein; 5 g carbohydrate; trace dietary fiber; 0 mg cholesterol.

Coconut Guava Cooler with Rum

This cocktail is light and refreshing, and it's a lovely shade of pink.

Ingredients

$1^1/_2$ cups (355 ml) guava juice

$1^1/_2$ cups (355 ml) sparkling mineral water

$^1/_2$ cup (120 ml) light coconut milk

3 ounces (90 ml) dark rum

4 lime wedges

In a pitcher, stir together the guava juice, sparkling water, coconut milk, and rum. Serve over ice in 4 highball glasses, garnishing each glass with a wedge of lime.

Yield: 4 servings

Each will have: 150 calories; 7 g fat; 1 g protein; 10 g carbohydrate; 4 g dietary fiber; 0 mg cholesterol.

Sangria

This is the perfect beverage to serve with Latin inspired dishes or just as an afternoon refreshment. It can be made a day ahead of time, if desired. Store it in the refrigerator and wait to add the ice and fresh fruit until just before serving. This makes enough for a party—present it in a punchbowl, if you have one, or a large pitcher.

Ingredients

2 bottles (750 ml each) dry red wine
2 cups (475 ml) freshly squeezed orange juice
2 cups (475 ml) unsweetened apple juice
$1/3$ cup (70 g) granulated sugar
$1/4$ cup (60 ml) freshly squeezed lime juice
1 orange, unpeeled and thinly sliced, for garnish
1 green or red apple, unpeeled and thinly sliced, for garnish

In a punchbowl or pitcher, combine wine, orange juice, apple juice, sugar, and lime juice. Stir until the sugar is dissolved. If making ahead, chill until serving time. Just before serving, add about 4 cups of ice cubes and float the fruit slices on top.

Yield: 10 servings

Each will have: 181 calories; trace fat; 1 g protein; 21 g carbohydrate; trace dietary fiber; 0 mg cholesterol.

Spiced Mango and Banana Lassi

Our take on the traditional Indian beverage is refreshing and deeply satisfying. It can even cure an upset stomach! Served over ice with a mint sprig for garnish, it makes a lovely beverage for guests at a warm-weather dinner party, especially if the menu includes curry.

Ingredients

2 cups (475 ml) lowfat cultured buttermilk

1½ cups (355 ml) mango juice

1 medium banana, diced

½ teaspoon ground cardamom

½ teaspoon ground cumin

Pinch of salt

A few grinds black pepper

Combine all the ingredients in a blender and pulse to puree. Serve with or without ice in tall glasses.

Yield: 4 servings

Each will have: 114 calories; 1 g fat; 5 g protein; 22 g carbohydrate; 1 g dietary fiber; 4 mg cholesterol.

VEGAN

Hot Honey Lemonade

This is a warming and immunity-boosting beverage that can help get you through cold and flu season intact. These amounts make 1 serving, but you can repeat the process as many times as you like!

Ingredients

1 tablespoon (15 ml) freshly squeezed
   lemon juice

1 teaspoon honey

Pinch cayenne pepper

Place the lemon juice and honey in a mug and pour 8–10 ounces (235–285 ml) boiling water over them. Stir until the honey melts, and add the cayenne. Sip while very warm.

Yield: 1 serving

Each will have: 25 calories; 0 g fat; trace protein; 7 g carbohydrate; trace dietary fiber; 0 mg cholesterol.

Homemade Soda

Instead of reaching for a store-bought soft drink, make your own soda by filling a tall glass with sparkling mineral water over ice and adding a splash of fruit juice or flavored Italian syrup. No recipe required!

Peppermint Chai

Our version of classic East Indian chai is not toothache-sweet, as so many commercial versions are. You can find all the spices at an ethnic market or herb specialty store, or order them over the Internet. Use rice milk for a vegan version—it won't separate when boiled, as soymilk is likely to do.

Ingredients

1 stick (4 inches, or 10 cm) cinnamon

8 large black cardamom pods

2 teaspoons fennel seeds

1 teaspoon whole allspice berries

$1/2$ teaspoon black peppercorns

1 piece (4 inches, or 10 cm) fresh ginger, coarsely chopped

2 cups (475 ml) lowfat milk or rice milk

2 green or black tea bags

2 peppermint tea bags

1 tablespoon (15 g) granulated sugar

Wrap the cinnamon stick in a cloth napkin and use a heavy object, such as a rolling pin, to break it into a few pieces. Place the cinnamon, cardamom pods, fennel seeds, allspice berries, and peppercorns in a saucepan with the ginger, milk, and 3 cups (710 ml) water. Cover and bring to a boil over medium-high heat. Remove the lid, reduce the heat to medium, and simmer for 5 minutes.

Turn off the heat, add the tea bags, and steep for 5 minutes. Strain the chai into a teapot or coffee thermos. Add the sugar and stir well to dissolve. Serve hot, or cool to room temperature and serve over ice.

Yield: 4 servings

Each will have: 116 calories; 5 g fat; 5 g protein; 16 g carbohydrate; 3 g dietary fiber; 17 mg cholesterol.

Honey-Streaked Latte

This beverage is a kind of free-form art when served in a glass mug—the honey streaks down the sides, creating unique patterns. If your honey has crystallized in the jar, immerse the jar in hot water for several minutes while you make the espresso. You want the honey to have a free-flowing liquid consistency.

Ingredients

2 shots (90 ml) hot espresso

1 1/2 cups (355 ml) cold lowfat milk

4 teaspoons honey, plus several drops

Brew the espresso and briefly set it aside. Place the milk in a cold stainless steel pitcher, and use the steaming wand on the espresso machine to heat the milk and create a layer of thick foam.

Place 2 teaspoons of honey in the bottom of each of two glass mugs and pour in equal amounts of the steamed milk, holding back the foam with the handle of a spoon. Stir to dissolve the honey.

Place a long-handled spoon in each mug, then spoon the foam on top. Pour a shot of espresso down through the center of the foam in each mug. Use a spoon to drip several drops of honey around the inside edge of the mug. The honey will run down the inside of the mug, forming interesting patterns.

Yield: 2 servings

Each will have: 124 calories; 2 g fat; 6 g protein; 21 g carbohydrate; trace dietary fiber; 7 mg cholesterol.

Almond Espresso Spritzer

This is a very refreshing coffee beverage. The orgeat syrup adds a hint of sweetness, and the club soda gives this drink a delightful effervescence. For a nutty-tasting variation, use 2 tablespoons (28 ml) vanilla syrup plus 2 teaspoons hazelnut syrup instead of the orgeat syrup.

Ingredients

2 shots (90 ml) hot espresso
2 tablespoons (28 ml) orgeat syrup
1 cup (235 ml) cold club soda

Place 1 shot (45 ml) espresso in each of 2 tall chilled glasses and stir 1 tablespoon (15 ml) orgeat syrup into each. Place 5 to 6 ice cubes in each glass. Pour $1/2$ cup (120 ml) club soda into each glass; it will fizz and form a foam cap on the top. Serve with straws.

Yield: 2 servings

Each will have: 44 calories; trace fat; trace protein; 10 g carbohydrate; 0 g dietary fiber; 0 mg cholesterol.

Brewed Coffee with Cinnamon and Nutmeg

Choose a medium-bodied coffee for this beverage, such as mocha java. The cinnamon and nutmeg fill the kitchen with a wonderful aroma as the coffee brews.

Ingredients

$1/2$ cup (50 g) ground medium-bodied coffee
$1/4$ teaspoon ground cinnamon
Scant $1/8$ teaspoon freshly ground nutmeg

Place the ground coffee beans in the filter basket of an automatic coffee brewing machine and sprinkle with the cinnamon and nutmeg. Add 4 cups (.95 L) water to the machine, brew, and serve.

Yield: 4 servings

Each will have: 1 calorie; trace fat; trace protein; trace carbohydrate; trace dietary fiber; 0 mg cholesterol.

Chocolate Raspberry Cappuccino

Berries and chocolate are a delightful combination. When you add them to a cappuccino, the results are delicious.

Ingredients

2 shots (90 ml) hot espresso
2 teaspoons chocolate syrup
2 teaspoons raspberry syrup
1/2 cup (120 ml) cold lowfat milk

Brew the espresso and place 1 shot (45 ml) in each of 2 warmed 5-ounce cups. Stir a teaspoon of the chocolate syrup and a teaspoon of the raspberry syrup into each cup. Place the milk in a cold stainless steel pitcher, and use the steaming wand on the espresso machine to heat the milk and create a thick layer of foam. Pour equal amounts of steamed milk over the espresso in each cup, holding back the foam with the handle of a spoon. Spoon the foam on top and serve.

Yield: 2 servings
Each will have: 62 calories; 1 g fat; 2 g protein; 13 g carbohydrate; trace dietary fiber; 2 mg cholesterol.

Hot Spiked Cider

Tuaca is a liqueur from Italy with a unique flavor; you may substitute apricot brandy if Tuaca is not available. This is a great after-dinner drink, in lieu of dessert.

Ingredients

8 ounces (235 ml) apple cider
3 ounces (90 ml) Tuaca
2 sticks (6 inches, or 15 cm, each) cinnamon
Lemon peel for garnish

Place the apple cider in a glass measuring cup and heat in the microwave until steaming hot, about 1 minute. Divide it between 2 brandy snifters and add half the Tuaca to each one. Stir with a cinnamon stick and leave the stick in the snifter. Use a vegetable peeler to strip off two long curls of lemon peel, and add one to each snifter. Serve very hot.

Yield: 2 servings
Each will have: 221 calories; 1 g fat; 1 g protein; 36 g carbohydrate; 7 g dietary fiber; 0 mg cholesterol.

Orange Spice Hot Chocolate

The orange extract gives this hot chocolate a wonderful, distinctive flavor.

Ingredients

$1/4$ teaspoon orange extract

2 tablespoons (12 g) pure unsweetened cocoa powder

2 tablespoons (25 g) granulated sugar

$1/8$ teaspoon ground cinnamon

Pinch freshly grated nutmeg

Pinch salt

$1^1/2$ cups (355 ml) lowfat milk

2 navel orange wedges

Place $1/4$ cup (60 ml) of water in a glass measuring cup heated in the microwave until steaming hot, about 1 minute. Stir in the orange extract.

Place the cocoa, sugar, cinnamon, nutmeg, and salt in a saucepan. Gradually whisk in the hot orange water, and heat over medium-high to a rapid simmer. Cook for 2 minutes, whisking constantly. Gradually pour in the milk, whisking to incorporate, and heat until steaming, but do not boil. Remove it from the heat and beat with an egg beater until slightly foamy, about 1 minute. Pour into mugs and garnish each mug with an orange wedge.

Yield: 2 servings

Each will have: 138 calories; 3 g fat; 7 g protein; 24 g carbohydrate; 2 g dietary fiber; 7 mg cholesterol.

Steamed Hot Chocolate

This is a coffeehouse-style hot chocolate, but it's simple to prepare at home using an espresso machine. If you have a can of push-button whipped cream in the refrigerator, feel free to top each serving with a dollop.

Ingredients

2 tablespoons (12 g) pure unsweetened cocoa powder

2 teaspoons granulated sugar

2 cups (475 ml) cold lowfat milk

Place 1 tablespoon of the cocoa and 1 teaspoon of the sugar in the bottom of each of two mugs. Place the milk in a cold stainless steel pitcher, and use the steaming wand on the espresso machine to heat the milk and create a layer of thick foam. (You may have to do this in two batches, depending on the size of your pitcher.) Pour about $1/4$ cup (60 ml) hot milk into each mug and stir to dissolve the cocoa. Fill the mugs with the remaining milk, holding back the foam with the handle of a spoon, and stir again. Spoon the foam on top and serve.

Yield: 2 servings

Each will have: 131 calories; 3 g fat; 9 g protein; 19 g carbohydrate; 2 g dietary fiber; 10 mg cholesterol.

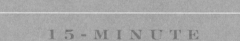

CHAPTER FOURTEEN

15-MINUTE
DESSERTS

Even when time is short, you can delight your friends and family with a 15-minute dessert. Chocolate is an almost universal favorite, and it stars in many of our recipes, but there are plenty of other delightful flavors here as well.

Some of our desserts are barely naughty in nutritional terms, while others are downright sinful. But sweet treats satisfy our primal craving for pleasure, and there's no virtue in constantly depriving ourselves. Make dessert an occasional special treat, and you can enjoy it without adverse health effects—and without guilt.

We haven't included any traditional baked desserts like cakes and cookies in this chapter—they just don't fit our 15-minute parameters. Our selection is therefore quite innovative and diverse, including Rum-Sautéed Bananas with Mango Sorbet and Almonds (page 222) and Green Tea, Gingersnap, and Coconut Sundaes (page 228). If you're a fan of ice-blended coffee-shop concoctions, you're sure to enjoy the Chocolate Malted Cappuccino Freeze (page 232).

There's a yummy dessert here for every taste and every occasion. Enjoy!

HERE ARE SOME CHEF'S SECRETS THAT WILL
TAKE YOUR DESSERTS OVER THE TOP!

Flavored Italian syrups, such as Torani, are tasty and versatile flavorings. They're available at well-stocked supermarkets or gourmet specialty food stores.

The pure, unsweetened cocoa powder called for in our recipes—sometimes labeled "Dutch process"—contains no sugar or other additives and has an authentically deep and complex flavor. Stored in an airtight tin in a cool, dry cupboard, it will retain its freshness for a couple of years.

Desserts are even more fun and festive when served in special small dishes or stemmed glasses.

Cream whips faster and has a fluffier consistency when you use cold beaters and a cold bowl. If you have time, place these implements in the freezer for about half an hour before whipping the cream.

Drunken Fruit Compote

This compote can be served warm with frozen yogurt, ice cream, whipped cream, or Light Crème Fraîche (see recipe, page 21). You even can spread it on toast for breakfast! Leftovers can be stored in the refrigerator and eaten cold.

Ingredients
1/2 cup (120 ml) spiced rum
2 tablespoons (36 g) orange juice concentrate
2 tablespoons (28 ml) maple syrup
1 cup (175 g) dried apricots, chopped
1/2 cup (75 g) dried figs, stems removed, chopped
1/2 cup (75 g) dried cherries

Combine 1 cup (235 ml) of water with the rum, orange juice concentrate, and maple syrup in a saucepan; stir to combine. Add the apricots, figs, and cherries, and bring to a simmer over medium heat. Simmer for 10 minutes. Serve hot, at room temperature, or even chilled.

Yield: 8 servings
Each will have: 152 calories; trace fat; 1 g protein; 31 g carbohydrate; 4 g dietary fiber; 0 mg cholesterol.

Bananas Sublime

This quick dessert will become a favorite.
The ingredients are easy to keep on hand.

Ingredients

1 medium banana, peeled and sliced
6 ounces (170 g) lowfat peach yogurt
3 tablespoons (45 ml) pineapple juice
$^1/_4$ cup (30 g) chopped almonds

Place half of the banana slices in each of 2
individual serving dishes. Top with equal
amounts of the yogurt, pineapple juice, and
almonds.

Yield: 2 servings

Each will have: 258 calories; 11 g fat; 8 g protein; 36 g
carbohydrate; 3 g dietary fiber; 4 mg cholesterol.

The Inside Scoop

For many people, ice cream is the
dessert of choice. Sometimes, its
combination of sweet, cold, and creamy
sensations satisfies like nothing else can.
To meet this demand, specialty food pro-
ducers have developed an abundance of
options. In addition to traditional ice
cream, supermarkets now stock reduced-
fat versions, sherbets and sorbets in a host
of flavors, frozen yogurts, and soy and rice
milk frozen desserts. When your next ice-
cream craving strikes, try one of these
healthy alternatives.

Rum-Sautéed Bananas
with Mango Sorbet and Almonds

This scrumptious dessert is special enough to finish off an elegant dinner party, especially if the menu has taken your guests to Mexico, the Caribbean, or the Southwest.

Ingredients

2 tablespoons (28 g) unsalted butter

2 large bananas, slightly underripe

$1/4$ cup (60 ml) spiced rum

2 tablespoons (28 ml) maple syrup

1 pint (300 g) mango sorbet

2 tablespoons (12 g) sliced almonds

Melt the butter in a seasoned cast-iron or nonstick skillet. Peel the bananas and cut them in half crosswise, then cut each piece in half lengthwise. When the butter is melted and barely sizzling but not yet browning, add the bananas and sauté for 3 minutes, then turn them over and sauté for 3 more minutes. Transfer the bananas to individual dessert plates and set aside.

Add the rum and maple syrup to the pan and bring to a simmer, stirring constantly until the liquid is reduced to a syrupy consistency, about 1 minute. Spoon the rum sauce over the bananas, then top each serving with a scoop of sorbet and a sprinkling of almonds.

Yield: 4 servings

Each will have: 190 calories; 8 g fat; 2 g protein; 21 g carbohydrate; 2 g dietary fiber; 16 mg cholesterol.

Healthy Banana Splits

Is this a fun breakfast, a wholesome after-school snack, or a delightful dessert? Whatever you call it, it's a great way to satisfy your sweet tooth and get some meaningful nourishment in the process. You may substitute other preserves, fresh fruit, and nuts to suit your own taste.

Ingredients

2 medium bananas

1 cup (245 g) plain nonfat yogurt

2 tablespoons (40 g) apricot preserves

2 teaspoons maple syrup

1/3 cup (50 g) fresh blueberries

1/3 cup (85 g) canned crushed pineapple, undrained

1/4 cup (18 g) unsweetened shredded coconut

Peel the bananas and cut them in half crosswise, then cut each piece in half lengthwise. Arrange 2 pieces side by side on each of 4 dessert plates.

In a bowl, stir together the yogurt, preserves, and maple syrup. Spoon equal portions of the yogurt mixture over each serving of banana. Top with blueberries and pineapple, then sprinkle with the coconut.

Yield: 4 servings

Each will have: 156 calories; 2 g fat; 4 g protein; 33 g carbohydrate; 2 g dietary fiber; 1 mg cholesterol.

Peach-Coco-Mint Sauce

The flavor of this sauce is light, bright, and refreshing. It's great on frozen yogurt, as described here, but you can also serve it on ice cream, or try it on sponge cake, garnished with fresh peach slices.

Ingredients

1 can (15 ounces, or 420 g) sliced cling peaches in light syrup, drained

2 tablespoons (28 ml) light coconut milk

1 tablespoon (18 g) frozen orange juice concentrate

6 large fresh mint leaves

1 1/2 pints (525 g) French vanilla frozen yogurt

Place the peaches in the blender and add the coconut milk and orange juice concentrate. Tear the mint leaves into pieces as you add them to the blender. Puree until smooth.

Scoop equal amounts of the frozen yogurt into 6 individual dessert dishes. Pour an equal amount of the sauce over each serving.

Yield: 6 servings

Each will have: 167 calories; 4 g fat; 4 g protein; 29 g carbohydrate; 1 g dietary fiber; 1 mg cholesterol.

Pineapple and Red Grape Parfaits with Granola

This dessert looks terrific built in a parfait glass or wine goblet. Make sure the granola you use is crunchy and fresh.

Ingredients

$2/3$ cup (160 ml) whipping cream

1 teaspoon granulated sugar

$1/2$ teaspoon pure vanilla extract

2 tablespoons (28 ml) pineapple juice (from canned pineapple)

$1/2$ pound (225 g) seedless red grapes

1 can (20 ounces, or 560 g) unsweetened pineapple chunks, drained (juice reserved)

1 cup (125 g) granola

Place the cream in a bowl and use an electric hand mixer or egg beater to whip it until soft peaks form. Add the sugar, vanilla, and 2 tablespoons (28 ml) pineapple juice and beat for a few more strokes.

Cut the red grapes in half lengthwise and place them in a medium bowl, reserving 3 whole grapes. Add the pineapple to the grapes and toss to combine well.

Alternatively layer the fruit, whipped cream, and granola into six parfait glasses. Repeat the layers, ending with a sprinkling of granola. Cut the 3 reserved grapes in half and top each parfait with a grape half.

Yield: 6 servings

Each will have: 164 calories; 6 g fat; 2 g protein; 25 g carbohydrate; 2 g dietary fiber; 15 mg cholesterol.

Ricotta Cheese "Fluff" with Raspberry Sauce and Chocolate Shavings

This rich and creamy concoction is not too sweet, but it's wonderfully satisfying. If you don't have a thick hunk of chocolate on hand, feel free to use chocolate chips or even cocoa powder in its place.

Ingredients

1 cup (155 g) frozen raspberries

2 tablespoons (25 g) granulated sugar

1 tablespoon (18 g) frozen orange juice concentrate

1 1/2 cups (375 g) lowfat ricotta cheese

1/4 cup (60 g) lowfat sour cream

3 tablespoons (60 g) honey

1 teaspoon pure vanilla extract

Pinch salt

1 ounce (28 g) semisweet or bittersweet bakers' chocolate

Combine the frozen raspberries with the sugar and orange juice concentrate in a saucepan. Cook over medium heat until reduced to a syrupy consistency, about 8 minutes.

Meanwhile, whisk together the ricotta, sour cream, honey, vanilla extract, and salt in a medium bowl. Mound portions of the cheese mixture into 6 individual dessert dishes and top with equal amounts of raspberry sauce.

Use a sharp vegetable peeler to shave the chocolate, and top the desserts with equal amounts of chocolate shavings.

Yield: 6 servings

Each will have: 220 calories; 8 g fat; 8 g protein; 31 g carbohydrate; 3 g dietary fiber; 21 mg cholesterol.

Raspberry Chocolate Fool

This is a pretty dessert, with the bright red berries standing out against the snowy whipped cream. Use homemade cookies or purchase your favorite variety from the store. You can whip the cream in advance; refrigerate it until you're ready to assemble the dessert. ("Fool," by the way, is an old English name for this style of dessert, not a comment on the cook!)

Ingredients

1 cup (235 ml) whipping cream

1 tablespoon (15 g) granulated sugar

1 teaspoon vanilla extract

6 chocolate chip cookies, about 3 inches (7.5 cm) in diameter, crumbled

$1/_2$ pint (125 g) fresh raspberries

4 sprigs fresh mint

Place the cream in a bowl, and use an electric hand mixer or egg beater to whip it until soft peaks form. Add the sugar and vanilla and beat a few more strokes. Gently fold in the cookies and raspberries, reserving a few raspberries for garnish. Place equal amounts in 4 stemmed glasses and garnish with the reserved berries and mint.

Yield: 4 servings

Each will have: 311 calories; 26 g fat; 2 g protein; 19 g carbohydrate; 3 g dietary fiber; 90 mg cholesterol.

Warm Berry Sponge Cake with Creamy Vanilla Sauce

Seek out a high-quality store-bought angel food cake to use as the base for this yummy dessert.

Ingredients

12 ounces (340 g) frozen mixed berries

$1/4$ cup (75 g) orange marmalade

$1/4$ teaspoon ground allspice

$2/3$ cup (160 g) plain nonfat yogurt

2 tablespoons (28 ml) maple syrup

1 teaspoon pure vanilla extract

4 slices plain angel food cake

Place the frozen berries in a saucepan over medium-high heat with the marmalade, allspice, and 1 tablespoon (15 ml) of water. Cover, bring to a rolling boil, and cook 5 minutes. Remove the lid and continue to boil rapidly over medium-high heat, stirring occasionally, until the sauce reduces to a slightly thick consistency. If the berry mix you are using contains whole strawberries, crush them with the back of a wooden spoon as the sauce reduces.

Meanwhile, whisk together the yogurt, maple syrup, and vanilla. Set aside.

Place slices of cake on 4 individual dessert plates, spoon about $1/4$ cup (75 g) of the berry sauce over and around each slice, and drizzle evenly with the vanilla sauce.

Yield: 4 servings

Each will have: 251 calories; 1 g fat; 6 g protein; 58 g carbohydrate; 3 g dietary fiber; 1 mg cholesterol.

Green Tea, Gingersnap, and Coconut Sundaes

This unexpected combination of ingredients puts a fitting end to an exotic dinner party. Serve it in glass dessert dishes or wineglasses to show off the colors. To make the gingersnap crumbs, fold the crisp cookies up in a cloth towel or napkin and crush them finely with a rolling pin or full wine bottle.

Ingredients

$^1/_3$ cup (80 ml) light coconut milk

2 tablespoons (28 ml) unsweetened pineapple juice

$^1/_2$ cup (45 g) coarse gingersnap crumbs

$^1/_4$ cup (20 g) flaked coconut

1 pint (285 g) green tea ice cream

In a small bowl, stir together the coconut milk and pineapple juice. Combine the cookie crumbs and coconut on a plate and toss until evenly distributed.

Place a $^1/_4$ cup (35 g) scoop of green tea ice cream into the bottom of each dessert dish. Top with 1 tablespoon (15 ml) of the coconut milk mixture, then 2 tablespoons (10 g) of the crumb mixture. Layer on the rest of the ice cream, coconut milk, and crumb mixture, in that order.

Yield: 4 servings

Each will have: 235 calories; 11 g fat; 4 g protein; 31 g carbohydrate; 1 g dietary fiber; 30 mg cholesterol.

Chocolate Soy Tapioca with Mandarin Oranges

It actually takes only about 10 minutes to make this pudding, but then you have to let it cool and thicken for at least 20 minutes before serving. If you want to make it ahead, refrigerate it until serving time. It's great either warm or cold. We highly recommend that you invest in a microplane, a handy kitchen gadget that makes quick work of grating ginger and hard cheeses and makes zesting citrus fruits a snap.

Ingredients

4 cups (9464 ml) plain soy milk

2 large eggs

$^1/_2$ cup (100 g) granulated sugar

$^1/_3$ cup (50 g) quick-cooking tapioca

1 ounce (28 g) semisweet or bittersweet chocolate, broken into a few pieces

Pinch of salt

Zest of 1 medium navel orange

1 teaspoon pure vanilla extract

1 can (11 ounces, or 312 g) mandarin orange sections in light syrup, drained (juice reserved)

6 tablespoons (90 ml) mandarin orange syrup (from can of mandarin oranges)

In a medium saucepan over medium heat, whisk together the soy milk and eggs. Stir in the sugar, tapioca, chocolate, and salt. Cook, stirring frequently to avoid scorching, until the mixture comes to a rolling boil, about 8 minutes. Whisk in the orange zest and the vanilla and transfer to a glass or ceramic bowl. Set aside to cool and thicken for at least 20 minutes.

Place equal portions of the pudding in dessert dishes and top each serving with equal amounts of mandarin orange sections. Drizzle a tablespoon of the mandarin orange syrup over each serving.

Yield: 6 servings
Each will have: 224 calories; 6 g fat; 7 g protein; 37 g carbohydrate; 3 g dietary fiber; 71 mg cholesterol.

Chocolate Sandwiches

This exceedingly rich and delicious dessert is inspired by classic French toast. The recipe is easy to prepare and sure to please! Garnish each plate with a fresh mint sprig, if you have some growing in the garden.

Ingredients

2 large eggs

2 tablespoons (28 ml) lowfat milk

$1/4$ teaspoon ground cinnamon

4 ounces (115 g) thin semisweet chocolate bar

4 slices sweet French bread ($3/4$ inch, or 1.9 cm, thick)

2 tablespoons (28 g) unsalted butter

1 tablespoon confectioner's (powdered) sugar

Crack the eggs into a large shallow bowl and add the milk and cinnamon. Whisk to combine. Form a sandwich by placing a 2-ounce (55-g) piece of the chocolate bar between two slices of the bread, making sure none of the chocolate extends beyond the edges of the bread. Pick up the sandwich and carefully dip it into the egg mixture to coat both sides well. Make the other sandwich in the same fashion.

Meanwhile, melt the butter in a skillet over medium heat. Place the sandwiches in the skillet and cook for 1 to 2 minutes per side, until the chocolate has melted and the bread is golden brown. Transfer the sandwiches to a cutting board and slice in half. Transfer each half to an individual serving plate. Dust evenly with the confectioner's sugar by placing it in a small, fine-mesh strainer and tapping the rim over the sandwiches.

Yield: 4 servings

Each will have: 302 calories; 17 g fat; 7 g protein; 33 g carbohydrate; 1 g dietary fiber; 122 mg cholesterol.

French Roast Ice Cream Float

If you have coffee left over, refrigerate it, and you can enjoy this float as a midafternoon snack. You may use any dark-roast coffee—French roast is especially good.

Ingredients

1¹/₂ cups (355 ml) brewed French roast coffee, chilled

1 cup (235 ml) cold sparkling mineral water

2 tablespoons (25 g) granulated sugar

¹/₂ pint (140 g) French vanilla ice cream

Scant ¹/₈ teaspoon pure unsweetened cocoa powder

Combine the coffee, mineral water, and sugar in a 4-cup (9464-ml) glass measuring cup or jar, and stir briskly to dissolve the sugar. Scoop equal amounts of the ice cream into each of two chilled 12-ounce (340-g) glasses, then pour in the coffee mixture. Dust evenly with the cocoa powder by placing it in a small, fine-mesh strainer and tapping the rim over the floats. Serve with straws and long-handled spoons.

Yield: 2 servings

Each will have: 185 calories; 7 g fat; 3 g protein; 29 g carbohydrate; trace dietary fiber; 29 mg cholesterol.

Chocolate Malted Cappuccino Freeze

Dessert and coffee all in one! Serve this bittersweet beverage to finish a summer dinner.

Ingredients

$1/2$ cup (120 ml) lowfat milk

1 teaspoon malted milk powder

2 teaspoons sugar

2 teaspoons pure unsweetened cocoa powder

$1^1/2$ cups (225 g) crushed ice

2 shots (90 ml) espresso

Place the milk, malted milk powder, sugar, and cocoa powder in a blender and add the crushed ice. Pour in the espresso. Cover and blend until frothy, about 1 minute. Pour into 2 chilled 10-ounce (285-ml) glasses.

Yield: 2 servings

Each will have: 62 calories; 1 g fat; 3 g protein; 11 g carbohydrate; 1 g dietary fiber; 3 mg cholesterol.

Minted Chocolate Milk Frappe

This is like homemade mint chocolate chip ice cream, but served as a blended, frothy drink. For a variation, substitute 2 tablespoons (28 ml) raspberry syrup for the mint syrup. Garnish with fresh mint, if desired.

Ingredients

2 cups (475 ml) cold lowfat milk

2 tablespoons (28 ml) chocolate syrup

2 tablespoons (28 ml) mint syrup

1 cup (150 g) crushed ice

Put the milk, chocolate syrup, and mint syrup in the blender. Add the crushed ice and blend until frothy, about 1 minute. Pour into 2 chilled 12-ounce (355-ml) glasses. The milk will settle to the bottom, creating a layer of froth on the top.

Yield: 2 servings

Each will have: 143 calories; 3 g fat; 8 g protein; 23 g carbohydrate; trace dietary fiber; 10 mg cholesterol.

Double Chocolate Shake

Chocolate and almond-flavored orgeat syrup are a marriage made in heaven.

Ingredients

$1/2$ pint (140 g) chocolate ice cream

$3/4$ cup (175 ml) cold lowfat milk

2 tablespoons (28 ml) chocolate syrup

1 tablespoon (15 ml) orgeat syrup

$3/4$ cup (115 g) crushed ice

Place the ice cream, milk, chocolate syrup, orgeat syrup, and crushed ice in the blender. Blend until frothy, about 1 minute. Pour into 2 chilled 10-ounce (280-ml) glasses and serve with straws and long-handled spoons.

Yield: 2 servings

Each will have: 222 calories; 8 g fat; 6 g protein; 34 g carbohydrate; 1 g dietary fiber; 26 mg cholesterol.

CHAPTER FIFTEEN

PREPARING FREQUENTLY USED INGREDIENTS

All of the ingredients used to make our 15-minute recipes can be purchased already prepared at supermarkets or specialty grocery stores. Keep in mind, however, that it's easy—though not quite as convenient—to prepare many of them at home, and the quality of homemade ingredients is often superior.

Here we offer some simple recipes for cooks who want to make rice, beans, or vegetable broth from scratch. They will take longer than 15 minutes to prepare, but the tasks are quite simple and involve little hands-on time. These home-cooked staples can be refrigerated or frozen for later use.

We also include here simple instructions for preparing a few specialty ingredients, such as roasted peppers and toasted seeds. These techniques are easy to master and soon become second nature.

The homemade ingredients included in the chapter will bring a special freshness to your daily meals.

Steamed Basmati Rice

You may prepare white or brown basmati rice using these directions. To enjoy basmati's characteristic light and airy consistency, rinse the rice before cooking, let the pot stand for at least 5 minutes at the end of the cooking time, and "fluff" the cooked rice with a fork after removing it from the pan. Basmati rice is a great accompaniment to curry dishes and light entrées.

Ingredients

1 cup (185 g) basmati rice

$^1/_8$ teaspoon salt

Place the rice in a fine-mesh strainer and rinse it for several seconds to wash off some of the starch that clings to the outside of the grains. Drain thoroughly.

Bring 2 cups (475 ml) of water to a boil in a medium saucepan over high heat. Stir in the rice and salt and return to a boil, then cover and reduce the heat to very low. Simmer for 20 minutes for white basmati, 45 minutes for the brown variety. Turn off the heat and allow the pot to stand without disturbing the lid for at least 5 minutes before serving.

Use immediately or store measured amounts in tightly closed containers in the refrigerator for up to a week, or freeze for longer periods.

Yield: 2 to 2$^1/_2$ cups (320 to 400 g)

Per $^1/_2$ cup (80 g) cooked: 123 calories; 1 g fat; 3 g protein; 25 g carbohydrate; 0 g dietary fiber; 0 mg cholesterol.

Steamed Brown Rice

You may prepare short- or long-grain brown rice using these directions. Because brown rice doesn't have much surface starch, rinsing is not necessary, as it is for basmati rice. Brown rice is a great accompaniment for hearty entrées.

Ingredients
1 cup (190 g) uncooked brown rice
$1/8$ teaspoon salt

Bring 2 cups (475 ml) of water to a boil in a medium saucepan over high heat. Stir in the rice and salt and return to a boil, then cover and reduce the heat to very low. Simmer for 45 minutes, then turn off the heat and allow the pot to stand without disturbing the lid for at least 5 minutes before serving.

Use immediately or store measured amounts in tightly closed containers in the refrigerator for up to a week, or freeze for longer periods.

Yield: 2 to 2 $1/2$ cups (390 to 490 g)

Per $1/2$ cup (98 g) cooked: 138 calories; 1 g fat; 3 g protein; 29 g carbohydrate; 1 g dietary fiber; 0 mg cholesterol.

Plain and Simple Cooked Beans

Black, garbanzo, cannellini, and pinto beans are the ones used most frequently in this book, and they are all easy to cook at home. The cooking time will vary according to the age, size, and variety of the beans. Give one a bite after they've been boiling for about 20 minutes, and be careful not to overcook them. They should be completely tender but not mushy and falling apart. Salting beans before they're fully cooked can cause their skins to toughen, but you may add other seasonings to the boiling pot if you like, such as bay leaves and crushed red chili flakes.

Ingredients

2 cups (455 g) dried beans

Before cooking, sort through the beans and discard any small pebbles or dirt clods, along with any beans that look moldy or shriveled. Rinse the beans well to remove surface dirt, drain, and transfer them to a large stockpot. Cover the beans with fresh water to a depth of about 4 inches (10 cm), then cover the pot and set aside at room temperature for several hours or overnight. (If you are pressed for time, use this shortcut method: Cover the beans with water as described above, then bring the pot to a strong simmer. Immediately turn off the heat and allow the beans to soak for 1 hour before proceeding with the cooking instructions.)

Drain off the soaking liquid and add enough fresh water to submerge the beans to a depth of about 2 inches (5 cm). Bring to a strong simmer over high heat, then reduce the heat to medium and simmer gently, stirring occasionally, until the beans are tender but not mushy. Cooking times will vary, but plan on 20 minutes to 1 hour or so. Check the pot and add more water, as needed, to keep the beans barely submerged.

When the beans are completely tender but not mushy, drain them in a colander (reserving the liquid in a bowl for another use, such as soup stock) and set aside to cool. Use immediately, or refrigerate or freeze measured amounts, submerged in cooking liquid or water in tightly closed jars. If freezing, leave about half an inch of headroom.

Yield: 4 to 5 cups (700 to 875 g)
Per $1/2$ cup (90 g) cooked: 129 calories; 1 g fat; 8 g protein; 24 g carbohydrate; 5 g dietary fiber; 0 mg cholesterol.

Vegetable Broth

This is a template for vegetable broth (or stock), not a recipe chiseled in stone. Any fresh vegetables you have on hand, including vegetable trimmings, such as onion skins and celery tops, can be added to the pot when making broth. Don't feel compelled to measure precisely— just use twice as much water as mixed vegetables by volume, and don't use too much of any single vegetable. If you include broccoli or other members of the cabbage family, keep their total quantity to no more than about 1 cup (70 g), as the flavors and aromas of such strong vegetables can dominate the broth. This recipe makes enough delicious vegetable broth for two or three great pots of soup.

Ingredients

2 medium russet potatoes, diced

2 yellow onions, diced

2 green bell peppers, diced

1 rib celery, chopped

1/2 pound (225 g) button mushrooms

1 cup (70 g) chopped broccoli

1 cup (20 g) torn lettuce leaves

6 cloves garlic, chopped

2 bay leaves, fresh or dried

2 teaspoons dried basil

1 teaspoon dried rosemary

1/2 teaspoon dried thyme

1/2 teaspoon whole peppercorns

3/4 teaspoon salt

Put 14 cups (3 1/2 quarts, or 3.3 L) of water on to boil in a large stockpot over high heat. Add all the vegetables, herbs, peppercorns, and salt and bring to a boil. Reduce the heat to low and simmer, uncovered, for about 45 minutes before straining. Discard the cooked vegetables (they make great compost). Any stock you do not use immediately may be refrigerated in tightly closed containers for several days or frozen for several months. If freezing, be sure to allow at least 1 inch (2.5 cm) of headroom in each container; the liquid will expand as it freezes.

Yield: 10 cups (2 1/2 quarts, or 2.4 L)

Per 1 cup (235 ml): 20 calories; 1 g fat; 0 g protein; 3 g carbohydrate; 0 g dietary fiber; 0 mg cholesterol

Avocados, Peeled and Diced or Sliced

Peeling an avocado as you would most other fruits is practically impossible. Fortunately, there's an easy method that won't even get your hands dirty.

Use a sharp paring knife to cut a firmly ripe avocado in half, lengthwise, all the way around the pit, then put down the knife and twist the avocado with your hands to separate the two halves. Hold the half containing the pit in one hand and gently yet firmly strike the pit with a sharp knife (be sure your fingers are out of the way!), then twist the knife slightly to dislodge the pit. Remove the pit from the knife by gently striking it against the edge of the sink or the rim of your trash can.

If the avocado is to be diced for a recipe, hold each unpeeled avocado-half in one hand and use the point of a paring knife to cut the flesh into uniform small pieces without piercing the skin. Use a spoon to scrape out the cubes. If the avocado is to be mashed, simply scoop the flesh into a bowl.

Herbs and Spices, Crushed or Ground

Whole spices can be coarsely crushed using a mortar and pestle. Place them in a sharply ridged bowl called a mortar, and crush using a heavy wooden or ceramic tool called a pestle. An electric grinder is the best choice if you want to grind a whole spice such as cumin or coriander seeds into a fine powder.

There are specially designed grinders for nutmeg and black pepper that will make quick work of these common tasks.

Small amounts of leafy dried herbs can be placed in the palm of your hand and crushed with your fingers before being added to recipes, releasing their flavors and creating smaller bits that will distribute better in the finished dish.

Nuts and Seeds, Toasted

Toasting adds a special depth of flavor to nuts and some seeds, such as sesame, sunflower, and pumpkin. Nuts and seeds require different toasting techniques.

You can use your oven (a toaster oven is perfect because of its small size) to toast nuts. Preheat the oven to about 350°F (180°C, or gas mark 4). Spread the nuts out in a single layer on a roasting pan and bake until lightly browned, stirring occasionally. Time will vary by nut, but begin checking after 5 minutes. Because they have a high oil content, nuts can burn easily.

To toast seeds, place them in a single layer in a heavy-bottomed skillet—cast-iron is ideal. Heat over medium heat, stirring or shaking the pan frequently, until the seeds are lightly browned and emit a pronounced roasted aroma. Pumpkin seeds will "pop" as they toast; this is a sign that they are almost done. Toasting times will vary by seed, but it generally takes only 2 or 3 minutes. Don't take your eyes off the pan, as seeds, too, are high in oil and are easily burned.

Peppers, Roasted

Roasted peppers are available in glass jars or cans at your local supermarket, but they're quite easy to make at home. Try it yourself when a bumper crop of peppers arrives in late summer in your backyard garden or at the farmers' market. You can use them immediately or freeze them to use during the winter months.

You can roast peppers using a grill or broiler or directly over a gas burner.

Preheat the grill or broiler, if using. Place the bell peppers directly on the grill, and grill for 10 to 15 minutes, turning frequently. (The skin will be charred black.) Transfer the peppers to a plastic bag, close the bag, and set aside for about 15 minutes. When cool enough to handle, peel off the charred skin and discard the seeds, stems, and white membrane.

Cut into strips or dice, as called for in the recipe. Refrigerate or freeze until needed.

Spinach or Other Leafy Greens, Washed

Many greens, including arugula and spinach, are now available prewashed and bagged, making them great convenience foods for busy cooks. However, if you grow your own or shop at the farmers' market, the fresh greens must be washed and bagged at home.

Fill the kitchen sink with cold water. If the greens have thick or long stems, twist or cut them off and discard or compost them (or rinse them well and save them for your next batch of homemade vegetable broth; see the recipe on page 239). Place the greens in the water, gently swirling them around with your hands. Allow them to soak for about 5 minutes so any dirt will settle to the bottom of the sink. Lift the greens from the water into a colander.

If using the greens immediately, spin them dry in a salad spinner. If refrigerating them for later use, drain briefly or shake to remove most of the water, but don't dry completely. Roll up gently in paper towels or a clean kitchen towel and seal in a plastic bag. Store in the crisper drawer of the refrigerator and use as needed.

Heads of lettuce can be handled in a similar way. They tend to be less dirty than spinach, so they don't need to be submerged in water. Simply rinse them well, shake off most of the water, and roll in paper towels or a clean kitchen towel before sealing in a plastic bag and refrigerating.

GLOSSARY OF
SPECIALTY
INGREDIENTS

Some of the ingredients used in this book may not be familiar to every cook, but are available in most large supermarkets. If you can't find these items in your local supermarket, look for them online or have a talk with the store manager, who will probably be willing to order them for you. If you live in a large metropolitan area, shop for ethnic specialty foods in the Asian, Mexican, or Italian districts of town. Your local natural food store is another great resource. You may be venturing out of your comfort zone, but such shopping excursions will greatly expand your culinary horizons.

BALSAMIC VINEGAR

This vinegar is quite distinctive, with a deep, pungent sweetness. True balsamic vinegar is produced in the Italian province of Modena using ancient techniques and is aged for many years in wooden barrels before bottling.

BASMATI RICE

This aromatic rice is available in white and brown varieties. Briefly rinse the rice before cooking for a light and fluffy texture.

BULGUR WHEAT

Bulgur is produced from whole-wheat kernels that are steam cooked, then dried and cracked into a coarse, medium, or fine grain.

CANNELLINI BEANS

These white kidney-shaped beans are rather nutty in flavor and hail from Tuscany. They can be purchased dried or canned at Italian specialty food stores and many supermarkets.

CAPELLINI

This very thin pasta can be purchased in dried form at any major supermarket, either coiled or in long strands. Fresh capellini is also sometimes available.

CAPERS

Capers are the flower buds of a Mediterranean shrub, usually sold packed in brine in glass jars. Sometimes capers are preserved in salt; in this case, they should be rinsed before using in a recipe. Capers have a unique piquancy that brings a bright flavor note to Mediterranean- style dishes.

CHAPATI

A chapati is an unleavened Middle Eastern flatbread that looks much like a flour tortilla made from whole-wheat flour. You may use it in any recipe calling for a flour tortilla.

CHÈVRE

Chèvre is the generic French term for goat's milk cheese. Fresh chèvre is soft and mild, with just a hint of tartness, and is widely available.

CHILI POWDER, PURE

Most commercial brands of chili powder include other seasonings such as cumin and salt along with the ground chiles. Our recipes call for pure chili powder, which is available in bulk at natural food stores or packaged in cellophane bags at Mexican groceries and some supermarkets. You can also purchase it online.

CHIPOTLE CHILES EN ADOBO

These are smoked jalapeno peppers, often sold canned en adobo—a rich sauce made from tomatoes, vinegar, and spices. They have a distinctive smoky flavor and are quite spicy, so a little goes a long way. Shop for them in Mexican markets and well-stocked groceries.

COUSCOUS

These are tiny beads of semolina pasta, originally from North Africa. They cook very quickly when soaked in boiling water.

CRÈME FRAÎCHE

This cultured cream is not as thick as standard sour cream, and it has a milder flavor. It is used extensively in French cooking. Shop for it in Italian specialty food stores or Mediterranean supermarkets, or try our quick homemade version on page 21.

CURRY POWDER

This exotic seasoning is a mixture of many spices and can range from mild to very spicy, depending on how much cayenne pepper is in the blend. The recipes in this book call for a mild curry powder. Sample different commercial brands to find one you like, or make some from scratch using the recipe on page 29.

DRIED TOMATOES

Also referred to as sun-dried tomatoes, they have an intense flavor and chewy texture. Dried tomatoes are sold as is or reconstituted in olive oil. If a recipe calls for the dried variety, it should be reconstituted before being added to a recipe. To reconstitute, place the dried tomatoes in a small bowl, cover them with hot water and set aside to soak for about 30 minutes (or place the bowl in the microwave for about a minute). Squeeze out most of the liquid and chop as called for in the recipe.

EDAMAME

This is the Japanese name for fresh green soybeans. They may be purchased fresh or frozen, in the pods or already shelled. Seek them out at well-stocked supermarkets, Asian groceries, or natural food stores.

ENDIVE, BELGIAN

These pale, cigar-shaped heads of slightly bitter leaves have a texture that is both crisp and velvety. They are available in the produce section of well-stocked supermarkets.

ENGLISH CUCUMBER

This variety averages about 18 inches (46 cm) in length and is sold shrink-wrapped in plastic. The unwaxed skin is very thin and mild tasting and the seeds are not large and bitter, so English cucumbers do not need to be peeled and seeded before you use them.

ENOKI MUSHROOMS

These pale, sproutlike mushrooms have small caps that sit atop long, leggy stems. They have a mild, almost sweet, flavor. They are best used raw or barely heated, as long cooking toughens them.

FERMENTED BLACK BEANS

Fermented black soybeans packed in salt are frequently used in Chinese cooking. They have a distinctive pungent taste; a little goes a long way.

GARBANZO BEANS

Also known as chickpeas, these round tan beans are sold both dried and canned. They have a nutlike flavor and firm texture that holds up well when cooked.

GARLIC

A pungent member of the onion family, garlic is available in many forms. In addition to fresh cloves, our recipes often call for crushed garlic, a convenient store-bought product ready to be measured out as needed, and granulated garlic, finely ground dried garlic without salt or other additives.

GINGER, PICKLED

Thin slices of fresh ginger that have been preserved in a semisweet vinegar brine. Look for a brand that does not contain food dyes. Our recipes call for the pale pink sliced variety of pickled ginger, not the bright red shredded variety.

JALAPEÑO PEPPERS, PICKLED

The pickling process adds a pleasant, piquant note to jalapeños and tones down their intense spicy flavor. You can buy them whole or sliced in Mexican markets or well-stocked supermarkets; the sliced variety are often sold as "nacho sliced jalapeños." You may remove the seeds if you prefer a milder dish.

KALAMATA OLIVES

Sometimes spelled "calamata," these succulent purple-black olives are native to Greece. They have an intense piquant flavor.

MIRIN

A sweet form of sake, Japanese rice wine, mirin is used extensively in Asian cooking. It is available in Asian groceries and well-stocked supermarkets. Dry sherry can be substituted in many cases.

MISO

Miso is a fermented soybean paste with a deep, savory flavor. Different varieties are available, some intensely salty, others with a mellow, sweeter flavor. Miso can be found at Asian markets and natural food stores.

NOPALES

These are the pads of the prickly pear cactus that grows prolifically in central Mexico and some parts of the western United States. They have a succulent texture and a distinctive fresh flavor with just a hint of tartness. Fresh nopales are sold year-round in most Mexican markets. Canned sliced nopales, called nopalitos, are more convenient to use; look for them in jars in the ethnic foods section of your supermarket.

NORI

Nori is a widely available seaweed sold in flat sheets in cellophane packages. Purchase nori that is labeled either "roasted" or "toasted" in Asian groceries and well-stocked supermarkets.

ORGEAT SYRUP

Almond is the predominant flavor in orgeat syrup. One widely available brand is Torani.

PARMESAN CHEESE

A fine aged Parmesan is straw-colored and has a distinctive flaky texture and nutty-sweet flavor that enhance salads, pastas, and many other dishes. It is readily available, either shredded or finely grated, in the supermarket cheese case, or you may purchase it in a block and prepare it as needed. We do not recommend the type of Parmesan cheese that is sold in a cylindrical container on the supermarket shelf.

PEA SPROUTS

These leggy, dark-green sprouts are mild in flavor and can be found at Asian specialty food stores and some farmers' markets.

PITA BREAD

Also known as pocket bread, this round, thin bread is available in whole wheat and white flour versions.

POLENTA

Polenta is dried corn ground into a medium-grain meal. Italian markets and natural food stores sell it labeled "polenta," but finely ground American cornmeal is the equivalent, and you can substitute it in recipes that call for polenta. Don't use corn flour—it is a different ingredient altogether and won't work in polenta recipes. Polenta is also available precooked, sold in plastic-wrapped logs in the refrigerator case of well-stocked supermarkets.

PORTOBELLO MUSHROOMS

These specialty mushrooms can measure 4 to 6 inches (10 to 15 cm) across and have a sturdy texture. They are widely available in grocery stores and Italian specialty markets.

QUESO FRESCO

This part-skim cheese has a mild flavor and a crumbly texture. It is used primarily as a topping rather than a filling, since it does not melt smoothly. Shop for it in Mexican markets or well-stocked grocery stores.

RADICCHIO

The radicchio called for in our recipes, radicchio de Verona, comes in smallish purple heads that are mottled with white. It has a pleasant bitter taste and is a popular ingredient in Italian cooking. Radicchio can be purchased at well-stocked supermarkets, specialty produce stores, and some farmers' markets.

RICE, WILD

Technically a grass seed rather than a rice, this dark—almost black—grain has a distinctive nutty flavor and chewy texture. It takes a long time to cook but is sometimes available precooked, packaged in vacuum-sealed bags. Check at your supermarket to see if they have precooked wild rice.

RICE PAPER WRAPPERS

Edible rice papers, or rice wrappers, available at any Asian market, are brittle and wafer-thin. Rice papers are sold in stacks, just like tortillas are. Soak each paper in hot water for about 30 seconds to make it pliable before using it to wrap up savory ingredients.

RICE WINE VINEGAR

This traditional vinegar has a delicate flavor that adds spark to many Asian dishes. It comes both seasoned and unseasoned. The seasoned variety is intended for making sushi rice. Our recipes call for the unseasoned variety.

SHIITAKE MUSHROOMS

These delicious fungi are available fresh or dried in Asian groceries and many supermarkets, sometimes labeled "black mushrooms." They have a potent flavor and chewy texture. The dried variety should be reconstituted before using. Place them in a small bowl, cover them with hot water to soak for about 30 minutes (or place the bowl in the microwave for about 1 minute). Squeeze out most of the liquid and chop as called for in the recipe.

SOBA

Soba are thin Japanese noodles typically made with buckwheat flour. For the best selection and price, shop for them at an Asian market.

SPROUTED-GRAIN TORTILLAS

These tortillas are 100 percent flourless, making them an excellent choice for anyone with wheat allergies. They are higher in protein and lower in carbs than standard tortillas. Look for them at natural food stores.

SUGAR, ORGANIC

Standard granulated sugar is sometimes bleached or processed with bone meal to brighten its color. We buy organic sugar to avoid these additives. Shop for it in natural food stores or other specialty markets.

SWEET CHILI SAUCE

This bright-red, sweet-and-hot chili sauce adds a distinctive flavor note to Asian dishes. You can find it in glass jars at any Asian market.

TAHINI

Tahini is a paste made by grinding raw or toasted sesame seeds. It has a texture similar to smooth peanut butter and a rather bland, earthy flavor that is best combined with piquant ingredients. Tahini is available at Middle Eastern markets, the ethnic section of supermarkets, and natural food stores. If the sesame oil rises to the top of the jar, recombine the tahini in a blender before measuring for a recipe.

TEMPEH

A dense and chewy "patty" made by fermenting whole soybeans, sometimes combined with rice or other grains. This high-protein food has a pleasant nutty flavor that combines well with Asian seasonings. When crumbled, it makes a great ground-meat substitute in chili and other dishes.

TOFU

Tofu is made from soy milk that has been coagulated to form curds. The blandness of this high-protein food makes it very versatile, as it readily takes on other flavors. Tofu comes in various textures, from soft and silky to dense and chewy, each variety suitable for different uses. Shop for tofu at natural food stores, Asian markets, and well-stocked supermarkets.

WASABI

Wasabi is a fiery-hot horseradish-based condiment that is best known for its use with sushi. It is commonly sold as a dry powder that can be reconstituted with water or rice wine vinegar to form a paste, then generally thinned with soy sauce before using as a condiment. The powder is sold in small tins at Asian markets and well-stocked supermarkets; prepared wasabi paste is generally packaged in a tube.

ABOUT THE AUTHORS

Susann Geiskopf-Hadler and Mindy Toomay have been cooking and writing together for two decades. Their ten previous book collaborations include *The Best 125 Meatless Main Dishes* and *The Complete Vegan Cookbook*

Susann is an avid cook who enjoys entertaining friends and family in her Sacramento Valley home. She does cooking demonstrations and occasionally writes seasonal food articles for a local newspaper. Her latest cookbook, *The Complete Book of Vegetarian Grilling*, was released in 2005.

Mindy is a writer, editor, and cook who plies the literary and culinary trades in Northern California. In addition to her many cookbooks, she is co-author of *The Writer's Path: a Guidebook to Your Creative Journey*. Visit her online at www.mindytoomay.com.

INDEX